A Life of Miracles

Mystical Keys to Ascension

Almine

Content Editor: Puff Anderson

**An Extraordinary Guide to
Living a Life of Mystery and Miracles**

Published by Spiritual Journeys LLC.

First Edition, November 1, 2002

Copyright 2002
By
Almine
Spiritual Journeys
P.O. Box 300
Newport, OR 97365

Content Editor—Puff Anderson

Cover Illustration—Charles Frizzell

Text Design—Stacey Freibert

Text Illustrations—Cara Anderson

Manufactured in the United States of America

ISBN: 0–9724331–0–4

Disclaimer

Please note that A Life of Miracles: Mystical Keys to Ascension is a documentary and reflects the personal experiences of Almine. This book is not to be interpreted as an independent guide to self-healing. Almine is not a doctor and does not practice medicine, and any information provided in this book should not be in lieu of consultation with your physician or other health care provider. Any reference to the word "healing" refers to the individual healing experience that a client may have had. Any reference to Almine as a "Healer" is not to be interpreted that she is a certified medical professional, or that she practices medicine in any way. The word "Healer" only appears as a descriptive term used for Almine, as she merely acts as a guide for each client as they work through their own individual healing experience. Almine, Spiritual Journeys, or anyone associated with this book assumes no responsibility for the results of the use of any technique described in this book.

In some cases, the names of individuals have been changed to protect their privacy.

Table of Contents

Acknowledgements

For their faith and unbelievable sacrifices to bring these messages into book form, my eternal gratitude to: Puff Anderson, who put her life on-hold for well over a year to gather the teachings from our vast collection of tapes and compile it into a book. She willingly did so without any compensation during that time. To Holly Berry, who has sacrificed incredible amounts of time and energy and worked for very little compensation due to her loving heart and extraordinary dedication to the project. To Charlie Sainz, who has run our office for three months without pay, to allow us to focus on this book. To Melanie Martin for the many hours given to help us with business advice and for holding the grander vision. To Margie Beatty for her never-ending love and support on many levels. A huge thanks to her and the Louisville volunteer crew who transcribed tapes. An extra thank you is extended to Arlene Courtney for reading the manuscript. To Jessie Morgan for his great spiritual insights. To Dr. Fred Bell, who has been instrumental in assisting us in the final stages of preparation, and most especially to my little girl, Jaylene, who is the light of my life.

Due to the purity of intent of those that have midwived this book into life, it is blessed. Those who have touched this work are the ones who have lived the teachings, and some have, consequently, already entered into God Consciousness. I am honored to work in the presence of such light.

With love,
Almine

Foreword

Perhaps it may have been the taste of the legendary apple in the Garden of Eden that gave mankind a conscience. It prompted awareness that there exists spiritual advancement beyond the purely animal instincts and material triumphs from the stone axe through to the modern super-computer.

Henceforth, there have been learned mystics throughout history who have pondered on this mystery of soul and spirit. Some were honoured and some ridiculed and reviled, yet we all know that somewhere the ultimate goal of peace, harmony and love exists. Through their teachings, these mystics have sharpened our conscience, whatever our religion, to seek the real truths beyond what the normal eye sees. In this age we are fortunate to have an outstanding mystic, Almine, who has dedicated her life toward this goal.

Clearly with Divine guidance, she leads us through extraordinary thoughts and meditations that will change our lives. She does not rely on flamboyant gestures such as extreme personal deprivation or living as a hermit. She lives among us as she teaches.

I have attended many of Almine's lectures and am always amazed at the immediate rapt attention of her audiences the moment she starts speaking. Clearly from her there is an aura of goodness, honesty, affection and truth that permeate the whole room. This is refreshingly different from the studied rhetoric of those, such as politicians, seeking to convince others for their own personal gain. Information from Almine will always leave one acutely aware and spiritually enriched.

This book will unfold a world of mystery and miracles and inspire you to reach this expanded horizon in your life. As one who has dabbled in the study of various Gnostic works, I am intrigued by the successful way in which the profound has been made understandable to all. It is a truly remarkable accomplishment by one of the leading mystics of our time.

The Right Honorable The 9th Earl of Shannon
Deputy Speaker of the House of Lords (1968-78)
Palace of Westminster, London, UK

Preface

There is a prophecy that says that the select ones from the holy races in the highest heavens will come down and walk amongst man. In 1997 when I was told to go out and speak publicly, I was informed that these would be the ones who would find their way to me.

I acknowledge your divinity and it is with great humility that I offer myself as a channel of light for these teachings. I do this in service to the glory of God—which each and every one of you is.

If even for a moment you have forgotten you are God, please know that I have not. These glorious beings of light who call themselves my students are the ones who have awakened me and reminded me of who I really am—a being as vast as the cosmos having a human experience.

So I present this sacred information to remind you of the magnificent beings you are. For it is in the flesh that the Divine is made manifest.

It is not my intent to tell you what I can do. My intent is to show you what you can become. My greatest wish is for you to stand on my shoulders and fly.

With love,
Almine

*This book is dedicated to
my beloved children
Monique, Almine Jr., and Brent.
Thank you for the privilege of being your Mother.
May you be unafraid to follow your hearts
for they lead us to our highest truths.*

PART ONE

A Life of Miracles

CHAPTER ONE

THE JOURNEY

The Gift of Life

It was during a South African spring that I arrived two months prematurely to experience a life filled with trials and tribulations, so that in overcoming them, I might show others the way. During the first few months of my life, my mother was twice awakened by a voice that instructed her to turn on the light and look at me. I had turned blue from lack of breathing so an around-the-clock vigil began at my crib. Many times I had to be turned upside-down and slapped repeatedly to bring me back from my travels into the spirit world. The doctors diagnosed these as crib deaths, and one such episode left me without life signs for several minutes. My parents feared not only for my life, but for brain damage as well. By the age of two I had also experienced eight severe kidney infections and ruptured ear drums. In exhaustion, my mother knelt in prayer and turned my life over to

God's will and safekeeping. Her faith allowed her to sleep peacefully through the nights, knowing that I would be cared for.

I spent a great deal of my first eight years sick in bed, with blankets piled high to break the fevers that seared my body. I contracted many childhood diseases such as mumps, chickenpox, and measles. I was forced to stay inside the house so I studied the beauty of the night and the passages of the sun and moon through my window to relieve the boredom. During these torturous hours I could hear other children playing happily in the gardens adjoining our home in Pretoria, South Africa. I wished to play too but the only way I could was to leave the discomfort of my body and astral travel around the garden. Only the dogs appeared to notice my out-of-body adventures.

During the rare and precious moments that I was well enough to be in the garden, nothing was overlooked. I knew each plant as an intimate friend and not one leaf was taken for granted. I knew the fragrance of each flower and exactly where the bullfrog, chameleon, praying mantis, and lizard lived. Much to my mother's dismay, I relished the smells and textures of the soil, of course, it ended up in my hair and on my face. During the summer thunderstorms, I sat in my little, wooden rocking chair bought from a peddler, and watched the heavy drops splash into the deep red soil. Keeping shoes on my feet was an uphill battle for my mother, as I loved walking on the verdant carpet of fallen Jacaranda blossoms and the fallen overripe mulberries that left purple stains on my feet. I learned that any day out of bed was a day to celebrate!

The South African educational system, while comprehensive, was very regimented and designed to intimidate and control through repression of individuality. My upbringing was steeped in prejudice, class-consciousness, and the fear instilled in the white people during the years of Apartheid. I had an inquiring mind so it was hard to accept the blatant incongruities in society. I studied world religions and since my parents didn't approve, I had to hide the books under my mattress and awake before dawn to study the world's scriptures. I did so until the birdsong outside my window announced the birth of a new day.

My health took a turn for the better following an incident along the Heunings River, where our family had joined other relatives for a large picnic. As the women laid out blankets and various delicacies, I found a perch on a mossy rock to peer into the depths of the pond at the foot of the waterfall. I leaned forward and lost my balance. The splash I made was drowned out by the roar of the waterfall. I found myself standing at the bottom of the pond in what appeared to be a golden bubble of light. To my amazement, I felt totally at peace. Time seemed to stand still, and I found myself breathing normally, even though there was no logical explanation for it. I sensed, rather than saw, a presence next to me. The question was asked, "Do you wish to live?" I thought of the joyous place and the Being of light that awaited me on the other side of the tunnel that I had gone through many times as a younger child. I thought, too, of my mother and father, their love and concern for me, and the grief my death would cause them. After some deliberation, I said, "I wish to live."

I was instructed by the presence next to me to raise my hands above my head and wiggle my fingers. At that moment, a cousin walked by and saw the fingers barely clearing the surface of the water. He called for my father who ran to pull me out. From that day on, my love affair with death abated and my health improved.

My mother once said that I saw "too clearly." I was continually taken aback by the facades, charades, and games played by the adults in my world. The cruelty of my peers towards others and myself, wounded me deeply, and my mother's aggression and prejudices seemed incomprehensible. I chaffed under the lack of grace, beauty, and sacredness in my environment, so I strived, in a childlike way, to turn my room into a temple. The adults jokingly called me a visionary, but secretly, many of them came to me for assistance to find missing valuables or to inquire which horse would win at the races.

At the age of 21, after the devastating loss of my father, I left South Africa to join my brother in the United States, where I would marry and raise three children: Monique, Almine, and Brent. Being a mother was a joy and taught me a great deal. Throughout the years of raising my children, I continued to search for the golden thread of truth throughout all the formal religions of the world, and I studied at Oregon State University between my second and third child.

While in prayer I asked God whether or not I should have a third child. A young man with a deep dimple in his right cheek, materialized in the room. He smiled at me and telepathically conveyed, "Mother, have you forgotten? Don't you remember all the plans we made? I am your son, and the time to conceive me is now." I decided to delay becoming pregnant to cleanse my body for this special child but he returned again and said, "Mother, I have a job to do. I must be conceived now."

I carried him 10 1/2 months and following his birth, when they laid him in my arms, my heart jumped in recognition. The following night, a being of white radiance stood next to my bed. The nurses would wake me every few hours to feed my infant so I asked them who this luminous being was. Later, it became evident that only I could see this holy messenger. As my son suckled his milk, I noticed the deep dimple in his right cheek and smiled to myself, remembering his appearance prior to pregnancy.

The sense of purpose Brent had prior to conception, remained with him. At the age of six, although fearful of dogs, he chose to walk home even though the school had warned that a vicious, rabid dog had escaped from the pound. When I asked where he found the courage to do this, he replied, "I know I have a job to do and that God wouldn't let me die so young."

These solemn insights and gems of wisdom came from all my children, and humbled me in the face of such innocent faith.

In 1987, as I reflected back on my life, I saw how many times my life had lain in ashes around my feet. Like the phoenix, I had risen and flown higher each time, but the essential purpose of life continued to elude me. For four days I sobbed to God, devoting many hours to prayer and refusing to eat. Finally, a soft whisper of my name shook me to my core. As I replied, "Master, I am listen-ing," information flooded my awareness. I began to understand that during my search for truth, I had missed the point: truth is what a master spontaneously brings to each moment, whereas a student spends his life searching for that which is outside of himself.

As I lay my questions at the feet of God, the answers gently came and changed my life forever. I told God that I refused to believe that the pain, death, illness, and separation I saw amongst humanity could be His will. I was assured that it was never God's will that we suffer. It was not His will that we beg for crumbs, for all that the Father has is ours. Therefore, we are to take our rightful position as heirs to the kingdom. It is in refusing to accept the appearances of limitation that we reveal the exquisite perfection underlying all things. A miracle is simply exposing this perfection.

"Where did these limited appearances come from?" I asked. I was told that we were created as creators; that our thoughts and feelings combine to shape reality; that death is an unnecessary accident that has always happened. It was through my refusal to accept death that I had opened the door to receiving information on how to overcome it. During the next several months the information poured forth and the right-brain way to overcoming death through ascension, was revealed in many different ways.

The day after I received the answer, I was having lunch in a bookstore deli and noticed a rather soiled version of Leonard Orr's book on immortality on the shelf. When I took it to the cash register, they had no record of the book, so the cashier sold it to me at half price. I took it home and read it cover to cover and placed it on the bedside table while I slept. That night I awoke to someone bending over me. The light was still on and as I opened my eyes, I yelled in fright. An East Indian man, who appeared to be a yogi, was standing next to the bed peering intently at me with his dark eyes. He ignored my fright and continued staring for several minutes. I stared back with open-mouthed bewilderment. Then he disappeared. Shaken to the core, I sat up and decided to re-read the immortality book as a way to soothe my nerves. I reached for the book and it was gone.

The following week a package of books arrived from De Vorss Publications in California. I was puzzled since I hadn't ordered anything. When I opened the package, it contained several books by Annalee Skarin. I called the publisher, offering to pay for the books. They had no record of sending them. I insisted that the postmark came from their town, so they reluctantly agreed to let me pay. "Could the author have sent them to me?" I inquired. There was a pause on the other side of the line. "Well, you see, she ascended into the higher realms followed by her beloved husband, Reason, after writing the first book."

During the next months I studied the sacred teachings that were camouflaged in a language that would induce an unaware or reactive reader to reject it. Clearly it was meant for those of discernment who could see between the lines. At times as I read her words, and as the Three Ascension Attitudes of love, praise, and gratitude became more understandable to me, I could hear otherworldly choirs singing praises to God. The cells in my body responded to the openings that were happening in my mind and heart. I could feel a perceptible increase in vibration at a cellular level. It felt like a refined and delicate trembling, so minute that it defies description.

Annalee explained how we become clothed with the garments of white light through the attitudes of love, praise, and gratitude representing the blue, yellow, and red colored rays of light. This was indeed accurate, for as I thanked God with all my heart and my cells sang in loving praise, there were times a soft radiance emanated from my skin. One such time occurred when I encountered my former husband's business associate. He looked startled, turned abruptly and left. He went straight to my husband and said, "It is the most remarkable thing. Your wife glows even in the shadows!"

I remember being in the Kensington Palace Hotel in London during that year. While in my room, my heart praised God for providing these sacred answers. Just then a visitor called from the foyer, and I made my way down. A dear friend, who had brought me roses from her estate as a welcoming gift, looked at me as though she had seen a ghost. "What's wrong with your face? You're shining like a light," she said and left hurriedly. I wondered what in the world she was talking about. One of the attendants in the foyer said, "My Lady, you're glowing, and where you are, there is no shadow."

During these months, I could feel my body undergo alterations. I would wake at night to find my bed shaking and my cells vibrating at a heightened rate. I told my children this was happening and they believed it was just my imagination until my daughter lay on the bed with me during one such occurrence.

In Annalee's teachings she gives a prayer entitled "In the House of My Enemies." She promises that when that prayer is prayed for one's enemy, that she and her husband would join that person in prayer. In 1989 I lost my temper with a business associate during a phone call. My cells had become used to the intense vibration of praise, so I immediately felt the energy drain out of my body, leaving me exhausted and weak. I sank to my knees next to the bed and recalled Annalee's prayer. As I prayed to God on behalf of my enemy, asking for understanding and light to come into his life, I felt the weight of someone's elbows next to mine and the gentle stroking of my hair. As I continued to pray, an arm reached around my shoulders and held me. At no time could I see a physical presence, but I am convinced that Annalee kept her promise. At that point I realized that the vibratory rate of one's body is more strongly affected by what goes out of it, than by what comes in.

As I changed during those years, my environment changed too. Both Brent and Almine Jr. were going through their own metamorphosis. Both of them decided to completely turn their lives over to God. One night Almine Jr. sought out the holiest place she could find—the stairs of a synagogue—in the middle of a large city. She sat huddled there for hours crying to God as she released her desires for specific outcomes in her life. She relinquished her will to God and lay her burdens at His feet.

I had become extraordinarily empathic and was able to feel everything. Consequently, I could feel her anguish even though she was 250 miles away. I wanted to console her, yet felt at a loss as to how. The next day I walked into a bookstore to buy her a music cassette, since music was an uplifting form of praise for her. While deciding which cassette to buy, I felt a powerful presence behind me. From the corner of my eye I saw a lady in a sky-blue suit, browsing near me. Suddenly she turned to me, and I glimpsed a diamond star on her lapel before she looked me straight in the eyes and said, "Tell your daughter she is never alone." Then she turned on her heels and quickly left the store. Several years later I saw a photograph of Annalee and realized it had been her in the bookstore.

The physical changes continued to accelerate and oftentimes I felt sharp pains in the heart, throat, and third-eye area. I was attempting, unsuccessfully, to succeed at international business during this time, an occupation that made it necessary for me to travel extensively. In every city my joyous heart sang its praises to God as I silently blessed and healed the multitude of people that walked pass me in the streets.

By 1992, I was 42 years old and found that most effects of aging were gone. In fact, there were times I was mistaken for my oldest daughter. It was during this year that I asked God to bring forth all remaining trials and tribulations at once. All I asked for was the strength to endure and overcome. I felt compelled to make this request because my yearning for full ascension (for my cells to become spiritualized) was so intense that I no longer felt at home in a world where death ruled. Even walking felt awkward. It felt as though I should be able to transport my body from place to place using thoughts. There were times, in states of great praise, when I felt completely light and wasn't fully aware of whether I was touching the ground or not. These incidents continued to grow in intensity.

Within 10 days of the prayer, one-by-one I started to manifest all my greatest fears: my husband and I decided to divorce; I lost my children (the greatest blessing of my life); I lost my beautiful, sacred home; and my income dwindled.

Within a few short months I found myself destitute and living on someone's charity in Salt Lake City. I tried to earn a living but I had been saddled with my husband's office debt and found myself having to live on $20 a week. That year the blazing summer turned into a bitter winter, and the small business I had started in Park City failed as blizzards prevented the usual flow of tourists. At night, as I cried out my anguish to God, rocking myself back and forth like a homeless child, unseen hands, again, stroked my hair. I lived in a tiny room in someone's garage with a mattress on the floor. Having had little exposure to extreme weather, I was mentally and physically ill-equipped to deal with sub-zero temperatures.

At night, while alone in my room, I managed to release my personal grievances by placing them in the hands of God, stating, "Thy will be done." As I fell asleep I often felt someone sitting on the edge of my mattress, though the unseen visitor never revealed himself or herself.

Taking advantage of my destitute condition, the older man who permitted me to stay for free in his backyard, started entering my room with an extra key in the middle of the night. He attempted to molest me so I ran outside in the snow, wearing only a nightgown, to escape his forceful advances. As a result, I contracted double pneumonia, and since I didn't have enough money for a physician, my condition deteriorated. (I later discovered that our bodies manifest that which isn't being expressed according to the will of our Higher Self. When the density of our situation stifles our lifeforce, it manifests in the respiratory system. That is why I had become seriously ill.)

I felt I had successfully turned over my hardships to God, all except Brent. He was the youngest and part of my very soul. Living without him wasn't negotiable. So after nine months of enduring separation from him, which I consider my "dark night of the soul", I checked myself into a motel to die. Yet, as I lay in the motel room, believing that the mere effort of breathing would end my life, I finally managed to lay him at God's feet. My prayer was, "Father, You have given Your son to show that death can be overcome and that we are masters of all things. I now give you my son to show you my willingness for Thy will to be done."

The room began to spin and I heard a voice instruct me to open the Holy Bible to Isaiah, chapter 54, saying that my life would be patterned after that chapter. Once the spinning subsided, I read it and began to see my life in its words. It thundered in my ears, "This is your prophecy." I read the passage again and again with tears flowing freely across my cheeks.

Suddenly I heard a bestial, clawing, and groaning at my door. I didn't know what it was. Yet a second later, angelic beings holding flaming swords of light appeared on either side of my bed. Overwhelmed by the situation, I fell into a deep sleep. I awoke several times in the night to find these guardian angels still present and the room lit with a glow emanating from them.

When I awoke in the morning they were gone, but a voice spoke loudly and clearly, "Gird up thy loins now, like a man, return to Oregon and take back that which is yours." Loading my luggage into the car and with just enough money for gas, I made my painful way back to Oregon. A journey that would normally have taken two days, took me six days to accomplish. I was so weak from the illness that I had to rest every few hours. It was March and snow still covered the prairies. I huddled on the rear seat and tried to cover up with my coat.

Something was wrong with my car so I asked God to help me make it home. In Oregon, a mechanic found that two essential wires had completely burned out. He looked at me in amazement shaking his head. "How could this car have run?" he asked incredulously. I arrived home weary, penniless, and announcing, "I'm here to stay."

In March of 1993, I moved back into my former house. By then my daughters were grown and had moved out. During the next several years I raised Brent and two other boys who were having family difficulties. The boys liked the peaceful and nurturing atmosphere of my home. After a long and tedious legal battle, I was able to retain the house and my son.

I started to teach the boys the information I was receiving through dreams, visions, and insights. Over a three-month period, I would occasionally hear the flapping of a bird's wings next to my pillow. God said it was the protection of a Native American shaman. In prayer I asked to see this guardian and a Native American, named Grandfather Stalking Wolf, appeared. During his infrequent visits, I became aware of the aliveness of all things, so everyday life became a holy journey.

Later we discovered that he had also taught Tom Brown Jr., who published several books revealing Grandfather's teachings. The books became a beacon of light to us.

These teachings prompted us to spend many hours in nature learning to feel the essence of the trees and rocks. On occasion we saw little elementals or nature spirits flitting among the trees.

Bathing became a sacred ritual as I acknowledged and thanked the water. I honored the fire as I cooked for my family and I blessed the food, thanking the spirits of the plants and animals for the nutrients they had offered.

While in prayer, I was taken out-of-body and found myself next to a blue, radiant pool of water. A female being, clothed in luminous foam and blue light, emerged from the pond and floated above it. She instructed me to look into the pond, and I could see the seas and oceans, the rivers and waterfalls, the clouds and rains pass before my eyes. I realized that all the waters of the earth were the physical manifestation of one grand archetypal spirit: the spirit of the water.

I routinely welcomed the rain spirit, knowing that the general consensus was that a rainy day was a "nasty" day and that this attitude must make her feel unappreciated. Due to my honoring the rain, she responded to my requests. I called upon her during times of drought or when we needed sunshine and she cooperated.

Due to the bond I developed with the water spirit, she responded to my emotions. The slightest upset on my part immediately caused water to spill or flow. On one such occasion, a parent of one of the boys came into my home and disrupted the sanctity we had created. I found myself becoming upset. That day the pipes burst independently of each other, on all levels of the house, flooding every floor. My insurance was canceled since the event simply couldn't be rationally explained.

Almine Jr. also experienced the magic of life. She spent hours every day worshipping God through song. Sometimes little balls of light would dance around her as she sang, and she knew it was a blessing from the devic kingdom. Brent was receiving a great deal of intuitive information, coming at such rapid rates that we hardly knew what to do about it.

As we were changing, so was the house, which seemed to have a life of its own. A rose bush in the garden burst into bloom even during the winter whenever a sacred visitor from the unseen realms appeared in the house. The roses were pinkish-purple and that color represents the divine love of Christ. Other times we could feel, but not see, the presence of a being of light, and with each incident, the house would make a loud whining noise with undeniable pops and snaps that traveled through the walls.

Many people have seen spheres of light in my home over the years, including Nick Bunick. Nick, whose experiences as the apostle Paul, written about in the book "The Messengers," came to visit with the author and publicist. As they sat in the living room, balls of light streaked across the room.

Unexplainable visitations by an array of masters of light started occurring, each one seemingly leaving behind a spiritual gift. I awoke one night to find an East Indian woman in a white sari, with a slightly chubby face and long wavy black hair, standing beside my bed. She was peering inquisitively at me. When she saw that I was awake, she ducked down beside my bed! In amazement I peered over the edge and she smilingly looked up at me, then disappeared. Soon thereafter, Almine Jr., through a series of miraculous synchronicities, became the student of the beautiful and beloved teacher Ammachi (Mata Amritanandamaya). I recognized her, from a photograph, as the woman who had appeared in my room.

Almine Jr., at this point, began to focus on the feminine principle of the universe, the Goddess. Frequently, walking into her home was such a sacred experience that I automatically went into an altered state. When Ammachi came to Washington, Almine Jr. insisted that her family be present during this first meeting with her teacher. She produced a sari for me to wear and had prepared a song and asked me to sing harmony with her. As I knelt for Amma's blessing, with my daughter in my arms, she raised up my head, and peering deep into my eyes, stuck a pudgy finger into my chest and said, "Amma, Amma, Amma!"—meaning mother, mother, mother! The intensity with which she said this left me wondering if she meant I was a mother many times over because of the extra children I had raised alongside my own, but somehow, I felt it had a deeper meaning. Little did I suspect that like Amma, I too would be blessing and healing the many that would come before me.

As my world became more mystical, it also became less accessible to others. The loneliness that summer engulfed me, so I traveled to the Grand Canyon in hopes of gaining some answers. After a long day's journey, I checked into a motel room and before sleeping, poured my heart out in prayer, saying, "God, I no longer fit with other people. Is there no one with whom I can share these spiritual experiences? Why are people becoming more hostile the more loving I become?" As I lay in the dark, I heard a voice say, "When you rise on higher thermals, like an eagle, you leave the flocks behind. The world knows that which is not its own and rejects those of a higher frequency." I understood intellectually what this meant, but I also knew that it didn't ease my lonely heart.

That night, unseen fingers were stroking my face and it disturbed my sleep. In my semi-awake state I thought I was dreaming so I made a concerted effort to wake up and end it. Yet even with my eyes open, the stroking continued. As I became more aware of my surroundings, I realized a large RV had been left running outside my motel room—its exhaust only a few inches from the intake vent of my room. In the heat of the summer night, the air conditioner had been sucking the noxious fumes into the room. By the smell, this had been going on for some time. I ran to the door and got help. In a state of shock I wandered back into the aired room and sat on the corner of the bed. I knew without a shadow of a doubt that I was never alone.

Over the years, I had an urge to alter every room in my house until it felt more like home. To my former husband's consternation, most of the changes were architectural. The result of this creative zeal is a truly unusual house. Little did I realize that the changes were to bring the structure into harmony with sacred geometry. Later I understood that sacred geometry is the lines along which Spirit moves to create and that certain measurements facilitate dimensional changes and energy vortexes that serve as

¿s between the realms.

Gradually, the wonders of the house have unfolded and I am still learning their mystical significance. The most sacred place of all is my bedroom, which is also a healing chamber. The ceilings slope up at 45-degree angles to a depiction of the transfiguration of Christ on the mount. When we change dimensions, light travels up the spine into the pineal gland, shoots out the back of the skull at a 45 degree angle until it is opposite the heart, then moves through the heart at another 45 degree angle. Dimensional changes, therefore, are brought about by a 90-degree change of directions done in two 45-degree angles. The geometry of my ceiling mirrors this so it facilitates dimensional changes.

There are 16 squares and circles in gold stucco bordering the image of the Christ, as painted in its original form by Raphael. The circle inside the square represents ascension through the balancing of the masculine and feminine components. In descending through the seven levels of the surface mind and the nine levels of the subconscious mind, we begin the ascension into Godmind. So, too, the Earth has had to move through 16 periods of descension to prepare herself for the glorious ascension that awaits.

All the masters of light that appeared did so at the same location in the room, and we believe it was the originating point of a loud explosion that startled the household. Following this unexplainable explosion that left no physical traces, the energy at this specific spot had changed. Our divining rods confirmed this, and when people entered the room, they seemed to gravitate towards that spot. Some explained it as feeling like standing in a warm, comforting light. Later I realized that during my remodeling, the room had been altered into a perfect golden mean rectangle. When this rectangle is divided into a square and another square, it forms another golden mean rectangle. Where these shapes meet, it creates a portal. Due to this, many of the sacred temples in the world use the ratio of the golden mean rectangle for their buildings.

The windows in the house were replaced by antique stained glass. Different colors are dominant as the daylight changes and each color seems to promote specific forms of healing. The windows at the end of the bedchamber have borders in the same colors as three energy fields surrounding the human body. Ostensibly the windows depict the four apostles after a painting by Albrecht Dürer; however, in fact they portray the four founders of Rosicrucianism: four immortal masters who brought information pertaining to this sacred brotherhood back to the earth.

The dark oak floors carry such a hallowed feeling that visitors involuntarily take off their shoes at the door. In amazing ways, pure silver items found their way into my home, as well as ancient books formerly belonging to the old alchemists (there are hidden codes in the pages). Their vibration added to the extraordinary atmosphere in my house. My home had become a temple.

During 1993 and 1994 my work was exclusively with my children and their friends. I was blessed with a large house that provided a haven for teenagers needing a place away from televisions, video games, or other electronic disturbances. The resulting amount of housekeeping was staggering, and I often worked from 6am to 10pm with little or no break. I decided to use my work as a form of worship, and like Almine Jr., sang songs unto God's glory as I worked. I noticed how doing something to the best of one's abilities—as a tribute to the Divine—differed from doing it from a sense of obligation. I began to realize that our worth lies in our attitude. The work itself is incidental.

In March of 1994, I voiced my intent to the Universe that I would love to take at least two of the boys to Hawaii for a vacation. The finances weren't readily available, but I decided to leave the details to God. One day later I received a call from a friend of a friend who said he worked for Pu'Uhonua Kanahele, one of the heirs to the Hawaiian Kingdom. His friends and followers called him "Bumpy". He had a vision that I was to help the Hawaiian people and represent him, and the other Kahunas, in Britain and Europe. They wanted me to come to Hawaii and bring the boys, and a hotel owner graciously volunteered a penthouse for our use. We found a bargain on airfare, and soon thereafter, we were in the islands.

The time in Hawaii was magical. I gave Bumpy a gift that Spirit had instructed me to take. It was a pendant dated by the Smithsonian Institute as being from approximately 300 BC. It came from the "mound builders" of Missouri. The pendant had a bear claw stained in berry juice and baked into clay. To my consternation, big tears rolled down the Hawaiian's face as he held it in his hand. "You have fulfilled a prophecy," he said. He explained further, "Many years ago my people went west in their canoes and then over land to Central America. They made their way north on a big river where they met people who built huge mounds. It was said that one day the circle would be completed by an item of theirs being carried back to the Hawaiian people. This would occur many years into the future. It would be a signal to the Hawaiians that their time of pain was nearly over. I am known as 'The Bear of The West.' By bringing me this object from the Mound Builders, you have completed the cycle."

Bumpy took me into the mountains to the sacred sites, where traditionally, only Hawaiians were permitted to go. The memories of that week enriched all our lives.

Soon after returning from Hawaii, on a stormy night, I was instructed by Spirit to drive two and a half-hours to Almine Jr.'s home to give her an initiation and blessing. Her dear friend, Lea

Ann, was there so I blessed her as well. I was inspired during the blessing to include her mother. Unbeknownst to me, her mother was ill, living in a different part of town, and at that very moment felt a surge of energy go through her body that healed the disease. Thereafter, Almine Jr., with friendly assurance, would advise people to visit me, "Oh, that's all right, my mother can heal you!" And so it began that I started working with clients.

The Gate of Power

Many visitors from other realms found their way through the dimensional gate that had opened in my healing chamber. In 1994, another gate opened and again there was a huge explosion without any physical evidence of a disturbance. This next opening occurred at the corresponding position on the golden mean rectangle but on the other side of the room, and immediately the energy changed. Again, our divining rods verified this.

The openings of my sacred spaces seemed to coincide with specific initiations in my life. One year later, I was reading in bed at midnight when a loud explosion reverberated throughout the room. This coincided with an experience where I was taken out of body and found myself standing with an angelic being before a very large gate. When I inquired about the gate, the luminous being explained that it was the third one on the path of ascension.

Apparently I had already gone through two other gates. The first was the gate of love. "The prerequisite for going through this gate," the angelic one explained, "is to see the innocence of all things. You pass through that gate only when you realize there is no good or evil."

Looking back I could see that Brent had grasped that concept before I did. He tried to explain it to me, but I couldn't quite understand. The insight dawned gradually that our true identity is a consciousness as vast as existence, expressing in human form. I came to understand that we aren't our experiences. We are all one grand cosmic being, expressing as many, having human experiences that were carefully designed by our Higher Self to gain insights. At times, we choose to experience life as the undeveloped light to gain perspective. It allows us to see who we are, by experiencing who we are not.

The result of this understanding has been that effortless healing takes place in my presence. The angel offered further explanation, "Once you pass through the gate of love, all your actions become more consequential. You start to make a bigger difference." I realized these insights had coincided with the first explosion that had occurred in my room.

"The second gate you passed through," the angel continued, "was the gate of wisdom. The prerequisite for passing through it is to be very still and very humble. You start to realize the necessity to hold on lightly to your belief systems; that today's truth is not tomorrow's truth." I came to understand that any one truth could only take us up one rung of the spiritual ladder, and those that claim to be masters for too long are stuck at the top of a rung. Having mastered a specific set of truths is an indicator to Spirit to knock us to the next rung, where again, we are students.

I realized I had ceased to strive. I seemed to effortlessly know all that I was meant to know at each moment. In fact, information came so easily it wasn't necessary for me to read books (something I used to love to do). I had become open and teachable, knowing that even a fool could be my greatest teacher. The angel further explained, "The requirement for stillness was fulfilled when you stopped striving. Instead of concern over the future, you lived spontaneously in the experience of the now."

I asked about the third gate. The angel explained that this was the gate of power and to pass through, it requires harmlessness and an awareness of the aliveness of all things. Respect for all of life was essential.

I found myself hesitating before this gate. Power wasn't something I had ever sought. I only wanted clarity and wisdom so I could selflessly serve all creatures on the planet. The angelic being spoke as though reading my thoughts, "It is in the flesh where the Divine is made manifest. Where God expresses there is love, wisdom, power and beauty. There are many that force their way through the gate of power using various mystical practices. But there is a limit to the power they can wield, for the universe doesn't entrust limitless power to one who hasn't mastered the self. Fear not, you have earned the right to walk through this gate."

In the months following my entry through the third gate, some interesting visitors presented themselves. I awoke one night to find a Scotsman in a kilt standing beside my bed. He had a wild, bushy beard and a rather austere—if not ferocious—appearance. He observed me a few minutes, then apparently decided to live in the house. Several visitors have seen him over the years. When I asked what his purpose is, he said he had made a blood oath hundreds of years ago and he is honor bound to protect the household. We still have the debatable felicity of his presence. We find that he is particularly active when we play old Scottish chants or bag pipes. He approached a visitor in the house and startled her. In a heavy Scottish accent he said, "Judging by your accent, you must be American?" This spirit can often be heard walking through the house, and on two occasions, has seen fit to hit someone through the face who was disrespectful to the house or myself.

One night I was awakened by the presence of an old man with white-gray beard and hair, dressed as a Yogi. He was carrying a water urn on his right shoulder. For many months I had no idea who this visitor was. Then one day I recognized him from a picture, as the founder of the Sikh religion.

The Egyptian god of the dead, Anubis, materialized in my room. He appeared about five feet, eleven in height. His naked chest was well built and he wore a toga that seemed to fold over itself in the front. His head was that of a stylized jackal. He stood beside my bed and radiated a bluish light throughout the room. His power was so potent, that I dare not stand, for it surely would have knocked me over. It was odd when he left that I felt a deep yearning for his return. His presence felt benign, and although his purpose was unclear, never before had I been in the presence of such pure, unadulterated power. A few months after his appearance, a black Egyptian Anubis dog woke me by placing his head on the edge of my bed. He wagged his tail and sat there as though waiting for a few pats. My heart filled with love for this beautiful animal, then he was gone.

Brent had found a mother tree in a nearby forest, and often went there for solace from the many visitors who came to our house. One night in the middle of a storm, he felt a persistent calling from this tree. He went to the forest and made his way up her rain-slick trunk to perch on a branch. During the next hours, he felt himself merge with the elements of the storm. He "became" the rain and then all the waters on the earth. He floated out-of-body above the forest and became one with the beautiful dance and interaction between the wind, water, and fire, for a rare lightening storm had begun. He could see the passionate dance of the trees as he moved through them as the wind. He could feel the lightening rip through his very being. He had become the storm. This occurrence established a mystical relationship between him and the archetypal spirits of the elements.

My physical changes continued and many nights I awoke with trembling limbs. One such night, I found two, white, glowing orbs hovering above me. When I asked God what they were, I was told the two beings had been assigned to monitor the metamorphosis of my body into an ascended being. They needed to ensure that my nervous system could accommodate the changes. Soon thereafter, I had an unpleasant burning in my limbs, particularly in the lower extremities. My children and I knew the Language of Pain so we rarely visited physicians because we understood the lesson Spirit was trying to get us to see by bringing on the ailment. When we embraced the lessons, the cause was corrected and the symptoms went away.

I spent hours of introspection, trying to find the lesson associated with this acid-like burning. It felt as though I had run a marathon, unprepared. For several years the pain intensified. At times I was so crippled that I couldn't trust myself to stand and maintain balance, even after sitting only a short period. It was a struggle not to limp as I walked.

I began to experience the value of living in the moment. For if I looked back over the several hours of agony, or looked ahead at the hours of suffering to come, I would have buckled under despair. As I sat shaking with pain, I consoled myself with the instruction that each second was new and that the only time I had to bear the pain was this second. I asked for healing and called from my heart for assistance, but for once in a long time, it didn't come. This forced me to work at maintaining a happy heart in the midst of this three-year-long trial. I asked that this fiery lesson leave me as pure as burnished gold.

Finally, in December of 1997, after a particularly harrowing day of burning agony throughout my limbs, I cried, "Why Father? Why am I experiencing such pain, and why can't I find the impurity within causing it?" I was told to go to the bookcase and pull out a little book, which I had intended to read for the last few years but had never gotten to. It was a book by Satprem containing interviews with a saintly woman in India, known as Sweet Mother of Pondicherry.

I opened to the exact page where she explained the burning pain in her limbs. She said it was the reason why the sages, Yogis, and Gurus throughout the ages had spent the majority of their time outside the body, traveling in the hidden realms. Being in the body burnt so unbearably that it would compel them to leave again to experience the realms of pure bliss. The Yogis called it "the sacred fire." Apparently the Yogic positions of the body were designed to gently stretch the muscles and alleviate this burning.

In Sweet Mother's life, she never found a way in the physical, to transcend this pain. However, she did find during elevated states of consciousness that it instantly disappeared. I found this to be accurate, yet I knew that not everyone experiences the burning. Even if they do, it can be transcended due to the tremendous increase in consciousness that is occurring each year.

I cried with gratitude to finally know the cause of what I had endured, yet I felt compelled to ask, "Why didn't you tell me what was causing this, dear God?"

"Because you never asked," came the response.

To my amazement, as I looked back, I had only asked for assistance, not inquiring about the cause. That taught me the importance of asking the right question.

Armed with this newfound knowledge, I again asked for assistance with alleviating this "sacred fire." Relief came within three days. I was lying on my bed waiting for a phone call, when I suddenly felt little darts of energy shooting into my body. It felt like needles and pins, but I could clearly distinguish that it was coming from outside my body. In my mind's eye I saw a drawing that I had once seen on an Egyptian scroll depicting an initiate lying on a bed, with a Priest standing behind his head, and tiny rays penetrating the initiate's body.

For three hours I couldn't move as these rays continued to bombard me. Abruptly, it subsided. My cells were agitated and I could feel a difference in their vibration as a subtle shaking. The pain was gone and didn't return again, except on two occasions when radionics were deliberately beamed at me through mechanical devices to lower my vibratory rate.

I felt as though I had emerged from a dark cave. Somehow I had passed my testing. I had managed to keep my joy amidst the pain and to remain patient and kind towards my loved ones. I am grateful for this suffering for it taught me self-discipline and control, the imperative need to live moment by moment, and the importance of making sure we ask the right questions.

Lessons from the Nature Kingdoms

The Bold Deer–As I became harmless, animals started responding differently to me. A deer walked toward me in spite of having to dodge rocks that were being thrown by an insensitive person on the hillside. She persisted until only 10 feet away and remained there until I left.

The Fanged Boa–One day at a pet store, I overheard the owner describe a boa constrictor from the Amazon jungle as a "real problem." He was a beautiful green tree boa with long fangs. The employees couldn't even clean his cage, since he would strike at anything that moved.

I grew up in an area of Africa that has 42 species of poisonous snakes so a fear of snakes had been deeply ingrained in me. I was eager to overcome this fear because it prevented me from becoming fully empowered. Consequently, I asked if I could touch the snake. The owner looked at me as though I were insane and told me to proceed at my own risk.

I took 15 minutes to calm my pounding heart and eradicate any expectations of failure from my thoughts. I visualized myself gently lifting the snake from his cage, with him responding positively. I spent another 10 minutes recognizing the divinity in all of existence, including this reptile. Finally, with a slow movement (so I wouldn't be mistaken for a bird, which is prey) I reached for the snake. Sensing no great agitation on his part, I lifted him out of the cage. I felt compelled to carry him to a distant part of the store where the fish were kept. My heart was still; the snake became still; and he seemed to enjoy my touch. I held him for about half an hour, marveling at his exquisite appearance.

When I gently placed him back in the cage, we both felt sadness at parting. I explained to the owner that the snake's agitation was due to the fact that his cage was too close to the birds, which placed him in a constant state of hunting due to the smell of his prey. I suggested that the cage be moved to a different part of the store to soothe his behavior.

The Day of the Frogs–While hiking one afternoon, I stopped to rest near a small muddy stream and decided to lie on my stomach and watch the frogs in their habitat. Initially they darted away, then I asked permission to touch them. As I reached out, one frog remained and allowed me to stroke his tiny back. It seemed to put him into a trance and reminded me of the way I kept Brent quiet in a grocery cart when he was a little boy. I would stroke the back of his neck with one hand, while loading the groceries with the other. He sat in such a state of bliss that the other mothers would look at me suspiciously, as though I had drugged the child!

The frog responded similarly, and eventually I reached around and stroked his belly. This went on for about 10 minutes. During this time, I telepathically received information from the frog. It informed me that frogs, through their songs, create a sort of doorway that allows other creatures to experience what it is like to be a frog. Also, the females judge the males by the strength of their songs, particularly the second "syllable" of the croak. Even though frogs generally start their song in unison, soon they begin to stagger the sounds in an attempt to drown out the second part of the others' croaks, in hopes that the females would hear their croaks. I was amazed that such brinkmanship would exist in the animal kingdom. I thought it was only characteristic of humans!

The Ivy–The garden surrounding my house had been tending itself superbly since I had requested that the nature spirit in charge take care of the flowers and plants. That year it was as though the garden had been fertilized and an abundance of flowers bloomed. I asked permission of the nature spirit to cut back the ivy from the top of the chimney as it had become a fire hazard. I indicated where I wanted to cut and waited for an answer. A cigar-shaped diaphanous cloud about 18 inches tall materialized three feet away. I heard permission being granted with the assurance that the ivy would withdraw its lifeforce from the branches that were to be trimmed. As I stood mesmerized, the little cloud moved to my right and then disappeared. (It was a clear day and no trace of smoke or clouds were visible anywhere.)

Due to the difficult location, I hired a gardener to prune the ivy. Even though I had given meticulous instructions, he butchered the plant. The nature devas must have rebelled because the next day, the flowers were dead. To my dismay, my magical garden continued to dwindle. I cried with remorse and buried several quartz crystals throughout the garden as a token of my love and appreciation for the work of the devic realm, but to no avail. The nature spirits didn't return that season.

The Blackberry Bush–That autumn I approached a blackberry bush in my back garden and was conscientious about asking permission to cut it back to acceptable proportions. Firstly, I shared my appreciation for its flowers and berries. Then I explained that it was blocking the sun from the other plants and snagging the sweaters of the boys when they mowed the lawn. I explained exactly where I would be pruning. As I listened for the answer from the bush, the following reply came, "In our kingdom we don't view death the way humans do. I am happy to recycle myself that other plants may grow—to retreat into the group soul and once again be born. This doesn't damage me. It is lack of honor and respect that damages our kingdom. We are called weeds and denied our place in the sun—our beauty and bounty unappreciated. I thank you for your consideration and appreciation. Humans are a synthesis of many different kingdoms. It is therefore through their appreciation and love, that a species is led to evolve into a more complex range of expression. Their acknowledgment brings healing and accelerated evolution."

I pondered the lesson of the blackberry bush, and it provided insights and wisdom to cope with an occurrence three weeks later when a man and his wife came for a healing. He asked her to wait downstairs while he counseled with me. As I spoke with him upstairs in the healing chamber I became aware of her growing agitation. By the time we went downstairs she was livid and loudly expressed her irritation. Having just come from a psychic session, I was highly sensitive and receptive and it hit me like a ton of bricks. I tried to console her, offering her a valuable gift that had been in our family, but she refused it. Then I recalled the lesson from the blackberry bush, and my frustration changed to compassion. She didn't mind being pruned out, but I had practically ignored her since I knew her husband was meant to be the client. Like the blackberry bush, she had become "prickly," yet she only sought acknowledgment and her place in the sun.

The Sand Fleas–I knew from experience that when I asked mosquitoes not to bite me, they couldn't be dissuaded from what they are programmed to do, namely, to suck the blood of warm-blooded mammals.

The beach where I routinely walked was invaded with thousands of fleas. They were so thick that the sand seemed to be in perpetual motion. An enmity began between us. I had to choose to either step on or carefully avoid them yet it was very difficult to miss the darting targets. Nonetheless, the carefree mood of walking at the beach was ruined. I wasn't sure if this type of fleas was bloodsucking or not, but memories of being bitten by fleas on the Cape Town beaches haunted me. I decided to fill my pockets with pebbles, tossing them three feet in front of me at regular intervals as I walked, sending the fleas scattering in all directions to clear the path. However, that took the joy out of the experience since I couldn't focus on the sunset, read the weather by the behavior of the seagulls, or marvel at the sandpipers streaking like quicksilver across the wet sand.

Finally, I decided to make peace with the fleas. I didn't know how a communication would go due to their seeming perpetual state of agitation, jumping up and down constantly. I knelt in the sand, acknowledging the divinity within these insects and the most amazing thing happened: the sand fleas congregated around me in a full circle (all their heads facing towards me) and all activity ceased. With an open heart and stilled mind, I telepathically communicated my appreciation for their role on earth. I received the information that they didn't suck blood, but helped dispose of the rotting seaweed. Their increased numbers were due to the increase in seaweed torn loose by the winter storms. I realized I could walk casually, ignoring their presence since they were far too quick and agile to be trampled underfoot.

I felt a great peace that stemmed from feeling like part of the whole. Man carries a heavy burden by believing we are separate from the rest of creation—not realizing the intricate way in which all consciousness is connected.

Feathers for Beauty–After months of being overcome by the glory of all lifeforms around me, I started wondering if I was beautiful too. I decided to take the matter to the Holy Mother, the feminine element of God. Surely She would understand such a question! I waited nearly three days for the answer. At the end of the third day, I was beside myself that it hadn't come. I decided to start the prayer over and was interrupted by a knock on the front door. When I opened the door, an irritated man, whom I had met once, was shoving an odd looking object at me. "Here are your darn feathers!" he blared. "I've been traveling to Sedona to give a lecture and for days Spirit has instructed me to turn around and head north and retrieve this object from my locker. Now I'm a full day late for the lecture I'm supposed to give." He looked accusingly at me as though I were personally responsible.

"But what is this?" I stammered, totally confused.

"When I made these three feathers into this prayer stick, the sacred geometry was revealed to me by the Goddess. I was instructed to prepare it for the highest ideal in female beauty. This is what Spirit has sent me to give you. Now may I please be on my way?" With that, he rushed off.

Tears streamed across my cheeks as I held the beautiful prayer stick, made with shells and feathers, in my hand. Surely this was the Mother's way of telling me to be still and know that I am beautiful too.

Messages from the Mineral Kingdom

In my interaction with the mineral kingdom, it is clear that the crystals and stones that have come to me in their own special ways, have chosen me, rather than my having chosen them. In 1994 on my birthday, I received two amazing crystals programmed with the knowledge of a Peruvian shaman. The following day I stood in prayer, a crystal in each hand, and offered my life to the service of God and all creatures on the planet. My head was thrown back with my eyes closed, when I became aware that the crystals had no weight. I couldn't understand this since they were large and hefty. I opened my eyes and looked down at the crystals. To my complete astonishment, I noticed I had risen several feet above the ground. Due to my shock, I fell down with a thud. To my unspoken question, the answer came as a small voice within, "Through the attitudes of love, praise and gratitude, you are set free from gravity and the resulting side effects of aging, decay, and death."

As I lay in amazement where I had landed on the floor, I pondered the extraordinary information which had been given, then Brent's voice called through the bedroom door, "Mom, Mary Beth is here to see you. She's waiting downstairs." I pulled myself together and made my way downstairs, but as I stood waiting in the living room there was no sign of her. Thinking that she must have forgotten something in her car, I waited. Suddenly we became visible to each other, and both of us jumped in surprise since we were standing several feet apart yet had been completely invisible to one another.

Mary Beth was so shaken that I led her over to a chair, and sat opposite her, trying to assure her that there was nothing to worry about. Even as I spoke she became more and more alarmed, clutching the arms of the chair nervously and looking as though she were ready to bolt. I finally realized that she wasn't listening to a word, so I simply waited for her to calm down. After a while a look of relief spread over her face and I suggested that we go into the kitchen for tea. After she composed herself, she explained that as I had sat across from her, I had disappeared again, and that time, only my eyes had remained. Through the eyes she had been able to see the starlit skies. She was so bewildered that she didn't visit long that day, but later on, we became dear friends.

Soon after my ecstatic experience with the two crystals, an uncomfortable feeling settled around the house. It grew so intolerable that Brent spent three nights camping outside in the garden. It was most intense in the healing chamber. My skin burned; my heart pounded; and a throbbing pressure was in my head. We couldn't think clearly while in the house. I suspected it was somehow connected with those crystals. I prayed, "Father, these crystals came as a gift. I ask You to help balance their energies so this household can return to its holy and perfected state."

The imbalance lasted three days, until a man named Jerry knocked on the door and said, "I have this beautiful, smoky quartz crystal I recently purchased, and even though I'm reluctant to part with it, it absolutely insists on living with you. Here, accept it as a gift. It belongs to you."

I placed the third large crystal with the others, and instantly, a peace settled over the house. The energies were again, harmonious, and my son moved back inside.

A week later, Jerry knocked at the door again, "Almine, I have been instructed by Spirit to perform a ceremony. I don't know what it is yet." I took him into the healing chamber and sat waiting. A strong energy moved through Jerry as he said, "The Masters of Light want to honor you this day for the work you have done. They lay roses at your feet." I could clearly feel something soft touching my bare feet as though invisible flower petals had made contact. A figure formed in the far end of the room, and I recognized the face of Mother Meera, a spiritual teacher. We both clearly heard the words, "Think of her as my sister," then she disappeared. Tears streamed down my cheeks as I realized this was the second sacred mother from India who had offered validation. I felt every cell in my body vibrating, and Jerry saw an exquisite pink-purple light gather around me and form a spiral that looked like a crown above my head. On my third eye, he saw a glowing blue star. (Many others have seen this star.)

There were many times when I felt discouraged, thinking my growth wasn't fast enough. I begged God for a physical teacher, wondering if that would speed my progress. The answer to this always pointed me to the verse that appears in I John 2:27: "But the anointing which ye have received of Him abideth in you and ye need not that any man teach you, but as the same anointing teacheth you of all things and is truth, and is no lie, and even as it hath taught you ye shall abide in Him."

I have been repeatedly told that although I am permitted to guide their lives, my children shall be taught directly by God. The appearance of Mother Meera in my room was further evidence that the sacred humans on earth, although separated by distance, were there to help us.

The Sacred Pools of Belize

Soon after my experience with Jerry, I had a dream that I was standing in a sacred pool in a river. As I held my arms up, a vortex of light formed and opened a gate above. In my dream I was dressed in a long white robe, standing in bluish waters. I was told that this was in anticipation of a trip I would be making to Belize, where an inter-dimensional gate was to be opened in preparation for the Earth's ascension. This would enable Beings of light to send their assistance to the planet and humanity. At that time, my finances wouldn't permit such a trip, but I left the details in God's hands. Soon after, I was informed by someone in England, that during a ball to celebrate Belize Day, they had entered my name in a raffle, and I had won a luxury trip to Belize, all expenses paid!

I bought a few new pieces of clothing for the occasion and departed from the Portland airport. Through peculiar circumstances I had missed my plane and had to take the next. As I sat down in the plane seat, I was thinking how God never wastes my time and that there must be a reason for this delay. I became aware of a wayward spirit in the vacant seat next to me. Apparently she had had a heart attack just a few hours earlier and had died in the seat. Her spirit didn't yet realize that she was dead and couldn't understand why no one could hear her and why people kept trying to sit on her. She was a frail elderly woman and was bewildered and afraid, not knowing what to do. With my intent I opened a tunnel above her and called forth angelic beings to escort her to the spirit realm. Within my mind I spoke to her, assuring her that this was the next step and it would bring her joy. My memories of passing back and forth to the spirit world as a young child helped as I explained to her what a beautiful experience it would be. I saw her leave, accompanied by two luminous Beings of light.

I spent the majority of my days in Belize searching for the beautiful pool I had encountered in my dreams. I trudged through the jungles and observed how nature's joyous chorus never ceased when the Indians entered the jungle. However, when one of the tourists entered the same jungle, by the third step, there was a hush as all animals halted their chatter and songs. I realized that the indigenous peoples of the area used the jungle's resources only when needed for survival. The urge to conquer nature—rather than cooperate with it—hung like a stench around most tourists. I admired the way in which reciprocity is the basis of the indigenous people's belief system. They give their thanks to the water, land and mountains for the nourishment and shelter they provide. This concept of reciprocity has too long been foreign to the mind-set of modern societies.

A native guide took me into the jaguar reserve. His job was to spot jaguars so he had developed a keen sensitivity. Therefore, I was puzzled when I heard padded footsteps following in the thick foliage behind us and he seemed entirely oblivious. I asked him several times if he could hear the sound. He looked at me as though I were crazy and simply shrugged. I decided to let him walk ahead and stood still to let the footsteps catch up with me. I turned and saw a beautiful spotted jaguar standing in the foliage. I stared mesmerized, noticing that it was becoming transparent. I was looking at a Spirit Jaguar.

It is said that the jaguar is the cat that doesn't roar, but I heard a sound, not with my ears, but rather felt it with my body. This inaudible roar seemed to change me, particularly affecting my root chakra. I knew that I hadn't been properly expressing the root chakra for several years, as I had lived primarily in the upper chakras. I felt as though an energetic plug had been released. The guide, busy swatting mosquitoes, hadn't noticed that I was no longer behind him. Finally, he became aware that he was neglecting his duties and came looking for me. I hurried on, shaken, but grateful for the gifts from the Spirit Jaguar.

The following day, I went on an excursion to an island with a group of people to snorkel. The guide looked at my faltering efforts at swimming with some apprehension, and after observing my attempts, said firmly, "Lady, just give me your hand, and I'll tow you around like a tugboat." As the Mayan man took my hand, a strong current of energy flowed through me, perhaps brought on by my intense joy over the extraordinary beauty of this underwater world. The effect on him couldn't have been more profound if it had been an electrical shock. He sank to the bottom, while I floundered at the top.

When he surfaced and regained his breath, he banished me to the beach. I sat there happily playing with the little crabs and looking at the diversity of the grains of sand as they reflected the sunshine. Eventually, the guide came to sit beside me, looking confused and bewildered. Clearly this wasn't an ordinary diving trip for him. To set him at ease, I started talking about the ruins that I was to visit the following day. Then he shared a story, "There is a legend that a blue woman will come from the south to open a gate that had been closed for thousands of years." He shook his head as if confused, adding, "I'm not quite sure why I'm telling you this."

He walked off to assist two other tourists. I continued amusing myself on the beach and pondered his words. Of course I wasn't that woman. Although I was from South Africa, I certainly wasn't blue. Perhaps it was a physical gate. I recalled having read that such a gate was discovered leading into the face of a rock cliff that seemed to be impenetrable.

I decided to play in the shallow waters where beautiful schools of fish darted around. I communicated that I wanted to swim with them and requested that they stay nearby. Suddenly I was surrounded by hundreds of little silver fish against my skin. They stayed in the shallow waters so I could keep pace with them. I stayed inside this school of fish for many delightful minutes, and it seemed as though I became one with them. They offered me a message, "All you know each day is that the current of life flows through that day. Cease to strive. Your only responsibility is to align yourself with that current and flow with the ocean of life. Pain occurs when we oppose life." I thanked them before parting company.

As I stood in the shallow water a moment longer, a group of pelicans dive-bombed the school of fish in the water around me, as though oblivious to my presence. Some of them struck the water about three feet away. I was able to observe this occurrence under water with my goggles. I was fascinated at how the school of fish conserved its energy. They didn't move until it was necessary to dart out of the way of danger. They didn't concern themselves about the next moment during this moment. This lesson was timely for me, since I had begun to be a bit anxious about the fact that I had only one day left and still hadn't seen the sacred pool.

As we left the island, a sudden rainstorm shed buckets of water on us. I was wearing a blue hand-dyed dress made in India that I had bought especially for this trip. The rain turned out to be more foe than friend on this occasion, since it caused the blue dye to run. It ran down my legs and arms, staining everything it touched. It was on my hands so as I wiped the water from my face, it became streaked. My long hair was hanging down my back so I ended up with dyed hair too. The other passengers were staring at me curiously, and I can't say I blamed them!

That evening I was dumbfounded that water could pull the dye from the fabric and spread it around, but water wouldn't remove it, even when scrubbed vigoriously with soap. Repeatedly, I showered and shampooed and bathed but I remained as blue as a Smurf doll. It was still there the following day when I traveled into the mountainous area to visit a resort. As I checked in, they explained that since there was only one other guest, they had upgraded me to a luxury, thatched house on the edge of the river. As I looked through the window of my room, I saw the beautiful pool I had seen in my dream. With my skin and hair stained blue, wearing a blue swimsuit, I made my way down to the river to open the gate.

As I stood in these sacred waters, I waited to be instructed as to how to go about the task of opening an inter-dimensional gate, but nothing was forthcoming. My joy overflowed, happiness streamed through every cell of my body and my heart praised God. Perhaps such joy would be enough to open this gate, I thought. But as I was in communion with God, tiny fish, that must surely have been cousins of the piranha, kept biting my arms. "Go away!" I ordered the little pests, "Can't you see I'm doing important work?"

Although I said this with a touch of irritability, I nevertheless understood the irony of my words, since I had learned that there was no important work. The little fish, however, were unimpressed and continued biting my arms. Finally I decided to move my arms in circles while in prayer. The clockwise and counter clockwise circles of my arms caused little vortexes to form in the pool and, combined with the strength of my emotion, the dimensional gate was opened. When I looked up I saw two moons, as well as many stars in the afternoon sky. At that inopportune moment, the one other guest chose to come down to the river and said with a heavy British accent, "How odd, there are two moons! I must go back and get my spectacles," and off he marched. By the time he returned, the two moons had merged into one, and I could no longer see the specks of stars. My happiness overflowed, as I had accomplished what I had come to do.

The next day as I left by plane, I was moved into first class, given chocolates and royally pampered. I took it as a message from the Universe that I had done well.

Messages from Spirit

On a glorious morning, not long after returning from Belize, I went for a walk on my favorite beach in Oregon. I sensed that it would rain even though there wasn't a cloud in the sky. The seagulls that were hunkered down, preparing for a storm, confirmed this. As I passed a group of them, I could clearly hear their communication, "There's a storm coming and you'd better get ready."

"There isn't a cloud in the sky," I replied, "besides, I'll be back long before it arrives."

About a mile down the beach, it hit. I got caught in a rainstorm that seemed to come out of nowhere. It turned out to be severe with blowing rain that was virtually horizontal. I became drenched and was chilled to the bone. As I struggled against the wind, not making much progress, I remembered the advice of the fish to cease to strive. I decided to sit down in the shelter of a driftwood log, and asked, "Ok, what lesson am I here to learn this day other than next time I'll listen to those darn seagulls!" As I stilled my thoughts, the answer came, "You are surrounded by energy. The entire universe is filled with energy that is available to you. Why do you choose to walk alienated from the power source that surrounds you? It is a universal law that you strengthen that which you oppose."

I took time to let the words sink in, and then stood and faced the storm. I felt the wind and the rain as they interacted with each other. I decided to stop fighting them and become part of their dance. I stopped opposing the cold and let it pass through me unhindered. I took my time walking back, feeling the thousands of droplets against my skin, drawing upon the strength of the storm itself. My walk began to feel effortless. A hundred little seagull heads watched my drenched and bedraggled figure as I walked past them trying to ignore their smugness that seemed to say, "I told you so".

Since then, when things aren't going smoothly, the first thing I ask is whether or not I am swimming against the currents of life. If I feel certain that I am moving in the right direction, I then draw on the energies of the universe.

It is interesting how Spirit had often used me as a courier. Sacred objects would come to me, but before my heart could embrace them, they would strongly declare that they weren't mine to keep. I was only safeguarding them for another that would eventually come along.

An East Indian man living in France had contacted me out of the blue. He said that he was in communication with an ancient Tibetan sage, known as the "Rat Sage." He had been told by the Rat Sage how and when to contact me. He was instructed to go to the city above the clouds, which turned out to be a small French citadel that sat on top of a mountain, like an island in the clouds. Once there, he was to find the House of Hawk. He made the trip to the little town by train and found an antique store by that name. Not having much money, he meandered around the store for an hour, waiting for some silent instructions. He noticed a small hawk carved out of bone or ivory lying in a tiny crack in the floor. He asked the shopkeeper the price. The shopkeeper said that there was no such item listed in their inventory, so he gave it to him for free.

He informed me that this would be coming in the mail, sent by the Rat Sage to be entrusted into my keeping. The hawk sat in my closet for several years, and I could feel its great antiquity.

One day my friend Mary Beth called and told me of an unusual incident that had occurred earlier that day. She said that a man had been driving down the road in his pick-up when a hawk swooped in front of his vehicle and did so repeatedly until he decided to follow the hawk, which led him straight to Mary Beth's door. His name was Larry. She somehow felt prompted to introduce him to me. I knew immediately that the hawk was his. Larry came to my house for a blessing and I gave him the hawk. Tears filled his eyes as he knew that he had carved it himself, many lifetimes ago. The hawk is worn around his neck in a little bag at all times—a wonderful blessing from the past.

Towards the end of 1991, I had become a shop owner. A rough looking man on a motorcycle pulled up to the shop, walked in, and handed me a small medallion with strange markings on it. He looked at me expectantly, as if there was to be an exchange. After a few seconds he said, "You have something for me." I instantly knew what it was, though I hated to part with the Egyptian scarab. While holding the scarab, his rough and wrinkled face melted and tears streamed across his cheeks. He explained that a surge of energy was moving through his body unlike anything he had experienced.

It wasn't until 1994 that I found the rightful owner of the strange medallion he had given me. Through a series of synchronicities, I was led to a tiny shop selling oils and tinctures. There, behind the counter was a bearded man with piercing eyes. The power of his presence could clearly be felt. I walked up to him and said, "Sir, pardon me, but this belongs to you. I have safeguarded it for three years." As he held it in his hand, he closed his eyes and stood silently for several minutes. I thought that perhaps it would be better if I quietly left since he was visibly moved. But as I reached the door he called me back. He asked me to step into the back of his shop for a moment. I obliged and he showed me a self-portrait he had painted of his Atlantean lifetime. He was wearing a robe of purple with a silver circlet on his head. He stood in a reddish circle that appeared to be made of stone. I pointed to it and said, "That is the circle of cinnabar the masters used in Atlantean times to travel between the worlds."

"Look closer," he instructed. I studied the details and there in his hand was the identical medallion that I had given him.

The Unfolding of the Gifts

I was often criticized for not asking for remuneration for my gifts of healing, which is a generic term for the many things I was instructed by Spirit to do. At one time I tried to ask for donations, since people were pouring into my house and I was feeding them, paying dry cleaning bills, and often allowing them to sleep in my guestrooms at no charge. However, I soon realized as my dependence on these donations grew that this was simply another way to have agendas with my "patients" - something I wanted to avoid at all costs. People would say there must be an exchange, but there always was. I received great lessons, insights and wisdom from each healing. In fact, much of what I now teach I learned from these healings. In this way, each person became my guru.

During 1995, I was working seven days a week, many hours a day trying to make time for all of the people (most of them Lightworkers) who were coming to see me. They came from all over the country. Some were unprepared for the extraordinary energies of the house. At this time, in the healing room a compass would simply spin round and round without finding north. These low or non-existent electromagnetic fields created the environment for increased access to Spirit, but at the same time, they brought people's unresolved issues to the surface.

On one such occasion, a man named Michael had driven many hours to come for a healing. I noticed that he was perspiring profusely. His agitation grew worse with every passing moment. Finally, he ran out the front door without a word, not even bothering to close the door behind him. Since I lived with these energies, I didn't realize just how strong they were to those who are unaccustomed.

This type of occurrence wasn't isolated and has continued to this day. I remember a young man becoming agitated in my house and it escalated into verbal belligerence. I was finally able to soothe him enough to get him to open up to the wonderful experience he was having. To his delight a ball of light manifested in front of him. Then he sat in the healing chamber for hours, allowing himself to experience the psychic abilities that he usually suppressed.

A man came to me that had multiple layers of trauma inflicted on him during his life. I thought it might be an extraordinary healing experience for him to spend the night in my bedroom so I volunteered to sleep in a guestroom. The next morning as Brent left for school, he looked into the bedroom, which the man had just vacated and saw an anomaly above the bed where he had slept. He called me and we saw a churning thundercloud of gray energy hovering above the bed. What had occurred was that the negativity of this man had manifested outside of himself during a spontaneous healing that night. The man was nowhere to be seen. The experience must have scared the wits out of him because he left without saying goodbye.

The advisor to Bumpy, the Hawaiian heir that I had visited in the islands, came to the house to experience its unique energies. I allowed him to sleep in my bedroom. He had been very bitter toward anything to do with Christ and tried to overlook the fact that he had come to what he described as a "Christos Mystic." I had written a prophecy for this man four years prior to meeting him. It had come during a vision. It touched him deeply when he read what I had written and how it coincided with his life. He lay awake pondering the prophecy and during the night he had a visitation from Jesus Christ. It completely removed the pain of rejection he had felt as a Jewish child, changing his life forever.

My mind was in such a constant state of praise that I often wondered whether I would disappear in front of my clients. Several have witnessed my becoming transparent, but I managed not to disappear entirely (that occurs when the cells of a body vibrate at such a high rate that it moves us into the next dimensional overtone). Once, while working with a college student, I noticed that the light changed to a golden color. Since he still seemed to be able to see me, I knew that somehow he had moved into the next dimension with me, but I decided not to say anything so it wouldn't alarm him. He started looking around and said, "Why, the light has changed in this room. Everything seems transparent...it seems as though I could put my hand right through the table next to me!"

I replied, "You can." The next moment he stuck his hand through the table, and due to his consternation, it immediately pulled us back into the denser reality. This experience was so disturbing to him that he had to rush to the bathroom to clean up his accident. That taught me not to push a student into an experience before he or she is ready. Even a miracle could traumatize. The instances of my becoming transparent in front of others increased, and I became the butt of many jokes among my family.

During prolonged periods of these psychic states, I often lost the ability to speak properly and my speech became slurred as though inebriated. There were nights it was so extreme that I wasn't able to take phone calls. I noticed, too, that I had an involuntary response of vibrating to the next level when threatened. One day, after hours of being in mystical states, I left to attend Brent's basketball game 30 miles away. When I got into the car, I was still in a state of ecstasy. I knew that I was late and wouldn't be there for the opening of the game, something that he had specifically asked me to do. I placed the matter into the hands of God. All I knew was that one minute I started my journey and the next minute I had arrived. It felt as though no time had passed.

I got out of the car and walked into the school while still in a heightened state. I thought the game was almost at an end, but I couldn't find Brent. Then I discovered that instead of being late, I was early. I was bewildered since the trip normally takes 30 minutes and only three minutes had passed on the clock. I sat on the bleachers in a dazed state and realized the miracle God had given me.

The competitive atmosphere and the roar of the crowd started to become overwhelming. I somehow interpreted it as aggression and could feel myself starting to vibrate out of this reality. This happened several times and I could see my son watching me intently.

After the game, he had a stern talk with me, " Mother, I love you dearly, but you aren't allowed to come to my basketball games again unless you stop disappearing off the bleachers." (Later I learned that by tightening the muscles right below my belly button, I was able to better remain in this density.)

I remember a day when a client stepped into the healing chamber with me and before I could even ask him to sit down, we seemed to be somewhere else. We could both hear the sound of Native Americans herding a stampede of horses. We felt the energy of the herd moving past us and could smell the dust, and hear the sound of their cries, and the thundering beat of the hooves. When I asked Spirit what had just occurred, I was told that we had experienced a part of his previous lifetime. He was so moved he could hardly speak. He had always been inclined towards Native American spirituality and way of life, even though he was a white fisherman in Alaska. This brought him understanding and illuminated his spiritual path.

Unfortunately, not all pilgrims to my house were equally respectful. One had driven up from Los Angeles for a healing. After having been in healing sessions for many hours, I decided that I needed some fresh air. I took him walking on the beach in the late afternoon and misjudged the remaining daylight. We found ourselves far away from the car as it rapidly grew dark. Oftentimes when doing spiritual work, strong emotions flow as people's hearts are instantaneously opened. These emotions can often be misread and he was falling into that category. He grabbed me and kissed me. I was so stunned that all I could do was cry to the Universe for help.

It was low tide, and the ocean had receded quite far. Suddenly, a finger of water reached out and slapped him in the back. The cold water startled him so that he let me go instantly. I darted away. As we walked down the beach, he was puzzled over the extraordinary phenomenon. He couldn't understand how the water could splash him when we were far from the water line during low tide. As we looked back, we noticed the marks of dry and wet sand in the moonlight, and clearly a finger of water about three feet wide extended about 100 feet out from the waterline. I silently thanked my beautiful and beloved ocean for coming to my aid.

The awakenings people experienced in my home at this time were so profound, that after healings we had to place them in various bedrooms to rest prior to driving. We jokingly called these "recovery rooms." It wasn't unusual for Brent to come home from school and find some bleary-eyed person sprawled across his bed. With his usual sweetness and beautiful nature, he took these things in stride.

Then there was the big excavation worker who came with his red suspenders and cork boots. He strutted into my house with his bushy beard and huge biceps. His name was David, and he came with the purest intent and humility of spirit, asking if I could open his heart. I did a healing as instructed by Spirit and told him that he would cry for several days to wash away the scarring of his emotions. Later I had a call from David and his tone was plaintive, "You've got to do something, Almine," he said, "I've been crying day and night for 13 days and the guys at work are starting to think I'm the biggest joke around." I was unsympathetic and instead felt overjoyed that this beloved man was able to release the painful baggage of his past.

Visitors of Light and Darkness

One of the benefits of healing work is that I was able to make many beautiful friends after years of living predominantly in solitude. It was around this time that I was pushed to meet a Lakota man who was called Walks with the Wolf. I was busy with a healing, and my client, as usual, was in an altered state. Suddenly, a Master of Light holding a violet flame appeared to my right and communicated telepathically that he was St. Germaine and I was to contact this man. I had heard of him and his teachings and tried to locate a mutual friend to obtain his phone number.

Soon after, I could hear a wolf howling around my house. The wolf calls continued until I finally received his number and left the following message on his machine, "I've been instructed by St. Germaine to contact you, and I believe that he has done the same with you, since I heard you calling around my house like a wolf. May I recommend that we talk by phone, instead?" We spoke not long thereafter. I had the additional privilege of getting to know the beautiful woman who walked by his side, whom I have taken to heart like a sister. They came to my home and we smoked his pipe. Although I had never smoked anything before in my life, and coughed all the way through the ceremony, they smiled kindly at my folly.

As time passed, my house and healing chamber grew more and more sacred. I prayed daily that I might heal as Christ did, without consideration of money and without agendas with the people who were being entrusted into my care. A friend named Amanda came, and I noticed a distortion in the flow of energy around her left-brain. Spirit told me that she had been blocking the sexual abuse that she had experienced for many years from a grandfather. I blessed her that this would release and that she might enjoy a healthy flow of energy unobstructed by memory blocks. By the next day, the release came and her husband held her as all the memories flooded back. Later, she became an invaluable aid and assistant to me for many months.

Emily, who was an artist, became transparent under my hands, as did a friend, Cara. Both of them radiated a soft glow until they left my house. Emily materialized geometric shapes of light in her auric field during the healing. Cara levitated above the table. The smell of roses clung to Cara for days, and even showering couldn't remove it.

I had a particularly strong connection with devotees of Parahamsa Yogananda, and each time I could clearly hear his messages for them. One young man came and asked me to interpret a profound dream. Fortunately, he was the last person I was seeing that day, as Yogananda stood by my side and gave him three hours of instructions that flowed so rapidly I could hardly relay the messages. The man was completely altered. It felt as if his life had been placed in perspective and his future became clearer.

A man named Andrew came with stomach cancer. He had managed to shrink it by treating it with wheatgrass and other raw juices, but he hadn't been able to eliminate it. By the time he came to me, he had made peace with his family, distributed his possessions to loved ones, and was preparing to spend the remainder of his days in Hawaii. I fasted and prayed for many hours prior to the healing. During the healing, I asked for his life to be spared and I heard the question: "And what will you give in return?" I thought of the love that I had for this stranger before me and without hesitation answered, "Father, through the love of my heart, I lay my life down for his." Andrew was healed that day. After he left, he called to ask if he was truly healed, and I reassured him. A few weeks later he went to a doctor in San Diego who confirmed that no cancer remained.

Andrew changed his name, and soon thereafter, the pain of his past was shed and forgotten. He became a wonderful healer and sacred languages flowed through him as he worked with people.

I learned the need to establish my recognition of the divinity within my clients before attempting to heal them. In seeing the glory of their true being, each one became as important as the living Christ. How could I not lay my life down for these glorious beings?

I had three visits by a broken woman who had suffered severely under years of sexual abuse within her family. Each time she came, I was compelled to stress the necessity for her to find her voice. I recommended that she start drumming as a way to express when words failed. She did and ended up organizing drumming circles for others. I had promised that when she found her voice, something beautiful would flow through her, and indeed it has. She is the author of a book containing messages from the archangels.

The profound changes I witnessed in my clients motivated me to keep working longer and longer hours. At this time, the Master, Jesus the Christ, began appearing in my home. Andrew saw Him standing next to the bed where he was lying in the guestroom. Mary Beth saw Him in broad daylight in the kitchen. While in a guestroom, Victoria was awakened by the bed floating as He stood nearby. Victoria also photographed the face of what appears to be Mother Mary in the windows in front of me while I was in prayer. The Christ also appeared to an Orcas Island woman who stayed at my house while I was traveling.

As I was standing in my bathroom one night, I experienced the loud snapping noises in the walls that we had experienced earlier. It was followed by a high-pitched whine, following the same pattern as the other incidents. I felt the overwhelming presence of perfect love and peace and fell to my knees. The soft light that appeared in front of me formed into a Being in robes of light. I bowed my head and felt hands on my head. I heard the voice of the Christ, which seemed to penetrate every cell in my mind, as he blessed me with words beyond description.

I found that not all questions were immediately answered because sometimes the answer was too complex for my understanding. Such a question concerned Lucifer and it took me a year to receive that answer. It was inconceivable to me that a universe made up of light and love could contain anything other than perfection. I was inclined to disbelieve that he existed other than in church teachings. However, after Lucifer appeared to both my son and myself, I knew otherwise.

During one visitation with Brent, although I was in a separate part of the house, I was aware that a great malevolent force had settled upon us. The next day my son shared the experience with me saying, "Lucifer tried to persuade me that to alter the universe and bring it into healing I had to join forces with his side. I tried to explain that there were no sides, that we were all one. I explained that my love extended to all creatures. The more I expressed my compassion for him, the more enraged he became. Finally, he left." Apparently Lucifer felt uncomfortable in the face of compassion.

Later, I received the following information about Lucifer and his role: A game of illusion was designed to help us gain perspective of our nature as pure light, by experiencing that which we are not. To assist with this game, one-third of the angelic hosts, under Metatron, played a neutral role. One-third, under Archangel Michael, did everything in their power to help us return to Source. The other third, under Lucifer, did everything in their power to keep us from returning to Source. The result of these opposing forces was the perfect timing of the birth of higher levels of awareness, much like a butterfly emerging from the chrysalis at the right moment.

I was told that the third that had volunteered to play the light retarders had no ability to feel. I wept for them, marveling at their courage to descend into density and forgetfulness where they aren't able to feel love or engage passionately in life.

Brent started receiving more and more information and oftentimes long mathematical formulas would come forth. He received information regarding the creation of the universe that would later become the basis of a body of information I would teach. At this time, he also started receiving the sacred geometry that pertained to left-brained ascension information, including the Mer-Ka-Ba activation. This information assisted the left-brain to remember the truths that the right-brain already knew.

On December 31, 1995, I was told to prepare myself to receive much of the history of the Earth over the following nine months. I had a feeling of anticipation and slight apprehension that night. I started to receive the first portion of the earth's history about a time when it was a large planet on the other side of Mars. I saw the creation of our solar system and the formation of creatures upon the planet.

When this information started coming, I was alone in the house. I heard a frantic scratching at my back door. A hostile presence was trying to enter the house, yet I also felt the protection of Archangel Michael, who guards my home. Before going to bed, I opened the window and called to the archetypal spirit of the Wind, asking her to protect my son for the night, since I could still feel that angry presence lingering outside the house.

Brent returned home and as he stepped out of the car that dropped him off at the curb, he paused in amazement. Although the night was calm and clear, a whirlwind seemed to surround him as though he stood in the eye of a miniature storm. It gently pushed him to the front door and stayed with him until he entered the house. The beautiful Wind spirit had done as I had asked and delivered him safely home.

A Sacrifice for the Planet

In January of 1997 I received the following information: "Prepare to offer your life for the planet in a sacred place, high in the peaks of the Andes on the 21st of March. A companion will travel with you."

I was confused. Was I to prepare a will and give up my life altogether? These questions remained unanswered. A week later in a dream, I saw a square slab of stone like an altar located high on the shoulder of Huyana Picchu Mountain facing the four directions. I also saw Larry's face, whom I had met briefly and had gifted the carved hawk statue.

I knew I was supposed to ask him to accompany me, but hesitated, knowing that he was a happily married man and that his wife could possibly take offense. I couldn't understand why God would choose Larry. He certainly was a beautiful, spiritual man, but his placid, benign demeanor didn't give away any clues regarding what special gifts he would bring to the occasion. I even thought that perhaps God simply wanted a witness to whatever was about to happen to me, so that my children, at least, would know. Somehow, the money presented itself (as I knew it would), and Larry's wife graciously allowed her husband to join me. Larry intuitively knew that he was meant to go.

The night before I left for Peru an ancient ceremonial pipe materialized in front of my bed, and I knew I would smoke it in the Andes on behalf of the people of the planet.

The farewell to my children had been difficult. None of us knew what to expect or whether I would be returning again. We only knew the command had been clear: go and offer yourself for the world. Brent's grayish green eyes looked deep into mine as he held my hands for a long time. Although he spoke few words, the look he gave me said it all. My eyes were brimming with tears, and I swallowed a lump in my throat as I left to drive to the airport.

It was awkward flying with Larry since he was a stranger. I still had no idea why he had been chosen, or why I was the one who had to lay my life down for the planet. However, my suspicion was that I had been one of the few who had volunteered.

As I sat on the airplane during that long flight, I thought about two potential problems surrounding the search for the stone I had seen in my dream. Firstly, I had a fear of heights. Secondly, since I was working too many hours each day, a deva had started untying my shoelaces, forcing me at least 20 times a day to slow down and tie my shoes. I tried all sorts of knots but nothing held and within an hour the shoes were untied again. People in the supermarket or on the street would see me running with loose shoelaces, and fearing the worst, would stop and bend down to tie them. I asked, "God, how am I supposed to climb those rocky ledges with loose shoelaces and a fear of heights?"

"Go to Condor Rock," was the reply.

The first day in Cuzco, Peru, was simply a time for adjusting to the altitude. It was so extreme that walking to the bathroom was laborious, and during the night the difficulty in breathing would wake me up.

That day brought an unusual welcoming committee. As I lay down for a nap, the flapping of a bird's wings around my room grew louder and louder, until it woke me. I sat up in bed and observed an outline forming in the room. It gradually turned into a male presence, an indigenous man of about five foot six inches. He stood staring intently at me. I sat, openmouthed, staring back and sensed somehow that he wasn't from the spirit world.

After a few minutes, I received a silent communication that he was a local shaman and had been told that I was coming. This was a projected image of his double, a concept I wouldn't understand until much later. He wasn't friendly or hostile, he was simply inquisitive. He stood for a few moments and then left. Not long after, I thought I heard another faint sound of bird's wings—large like a condor. This time an entirely different male figure appeared in the room. His message was basically the same: he had been told about my arrival and my mission, and he had come to look at my heart. However, I did get a feeling of support from this projection of a living shaman.

The second day in Cuzco, I had an out-of-body experience just before dawn. I felt myself rise up above my body and transport in a swirling mist to another location. I found myself amongst ruins of red stones and noticed how the windows of this ancient civilization's building were aligned with the path of the rising sun. I cried for the Earth, prostrate before the rising sun, and my tears flowed into the red soil as I called upon the Creator to intervene on behalf of the planet.

The next day our guide introduced himself, and Larry and I set out on our first excursion. He called himself Farrah, yet his given name meant "Messenger of the Gods." He was a beautiful spiritual man. Often as we shared our sacred experiences, his tears of devotion would freely flow. Farrah's love for Mother Earth, Pachamama, was evident, and he walked reverently on the land. It was clear to me why God had chosen him to be part of this sacred journey.

One of the places Farrah took us was Condor Rock. This rock loomed high above a small village that lay in the silence of the ages. He knew things about these sacred sites that archeologists didn't know. He asked if I wanted to sit on the back of Condor Rock. Knowing that it was meant to be, I gingerly made my way to the top, loose shoelaces and all. I wasn't very high, yet my knees were already a little shaky. (I wished for an instant that I had swallowed my pride and gotten Velcro closure shoes!)

I sat on top of the rock with my eyes closed so as not to see the distance below. I called with all my might to the spirit of the condor to enter my body and make me comfortable with heights. Suddenly, a breeze blew around me and it felt as though I had taken flight. I could feel the wind through my feathers and the quivering of the air beneath my wings. The majestic spirit of this huge bird, so revered by the indigenous people, flowed through me. Then I was jolted back to this reality.

The climb down was much easier. My experience on the rock

was unspeakable so I couldn't bring myself to share it with my traveling partners. My shoelaces continued to be untied, even though Larry patiently tried the best Boy Scout knots he knew. To my astonishment, I was able to complete the remainder of the hike with surefootedness and a complete lack of fear.

One morning, with a picnic lunch in Farrah's backpack, we climbed for about an hour. Suddenly, a large eagle swooped overhead, and three times dived down directly in front of us, across our path. The guide stoically marched ahead, but Larry and I were having difficulty with the altitude. I stood for a moment to catch my breath and tried to understand the message of the eagle. Then a brightly colored hummingbird flew up to my face and, darting forward, stuck his long beak in my mouth. Larry saw it too, and we both were taken aback. I asked Farrah about it and he explained that, in Incalore, the kiss of a hummingbird was an initiation.

As I rounded the next bend, I saw the red-stoned ruins that I had seen during my out-of-body travels a few days before. I lay down on the ground, facing the East and cried for the atrocities that were committed against our beloved Mother Earth. When we smoked my pipe and Farrah burned his special incense, the birds in the area gathered near for the sacred ceremony.

The time was nearing for me to travel with Larry to Machu Picchu and although the sacred experiences of these days were rich, like golden threads in the tapestry of my life, the impatience for what was to come grew inside me. I had trained my mind not to indulge in speculation or self-analysis. The years of alternating between deep spiritual experiences and daily responsibilities— running to the grocery store, then returning to participate in an out-of-body experience with a client—taught me to live in the moment. I used this discipline to banish any fear that arose concerning what my forthcoming sacrifice on Machu Picchu would entail.

The thought of not returning home made me appreciate the smells of the earth, the songs of the birds, and the field flowers a hundred times more. I promised myself that whatever happened, I would strive to live the rest of my days in such a state of heightened awareness.

The 20th of March came, and with it, our first visit to Machu Picchu. Farrah showed us where underground caverns existed. He had us place our heads in niches in a wall and chant, explaining that the caverns were constructed for the purpose of clearing the chakras of debris when initiates did this exercise. We performed a ceremony to honor the spirits of this pilgrimage site, using cocoa leaves as our gift of gratitude (the same as Native Americans would use tobacco).

A presence came through Larry while in prayer. He spoke with force and called upon Pan, the great nature custodian. His casual air was completely transformed to one of power. Now I understood that God had chosen Larry because of his mystical connection with the nature spirit who guarded the plants and animals of the Earth. I had felt isolated and unprepared for this awesome task, but I could see that my travelling partners and beings from the unseen realms were offering their support.

On the 21st of March we arrived at Machu Picchu before dawn. By midmorning we had made our way to the rock that resembles a condor, overlooking the city. As we made our sacred circle and set out our incense, tobacco, cocoa leaves, and my pipe, two huge condors circled above. Farrah instantly became overcome with emotion. I was impressed, as I had never seen condors before. He lived in this area so I thought this must surely be a common sight. Yet his eyes grew big and tears started flowing across his cheeks as he held his hands up to honor the great birds. For many years he had studied the interpretation of the condor's movements according to shamanic lore. He intently studied the pair near us and translated their message. He said it was an omen—an auspicious sign that an important event was about to happen. He noticed that many unseen beings stood nearby, ready to assist me. The Spirits had accepted our reverence for the holy site and the mission would be successful.

Farrah paused and looked upward and as though that had been their cue, the condors rose higher and higher and glided away.

Below us the ruins of Machu Picchu straddled the mountain, and I noticed the stream of tourists making their way to the site. I wished with all my heart that we could have some privacy. I closed my eyes and began to pray. Larry followed suit. With a majestic presence he spoke, imploring the divine assistance of the heavens. Within minutes, a cloud covering spread itself to cover the ruins below. Our area remained clear like an island in the sky. I had instantly been granted the privacy I had requested.

We smoked my pipe. The correct way this sacred object was to be used came effortlessly through me, as though I had been doing it for centuries.

When our ceremony was over, it was about 11 a.m. when I had a sudden urge to move on. Loose shoelaces not withstanding, I clambered higher as though compelled. My odd behavior left my partners perplexed. I didn't try to explain, but kept climbing. Finally, I found myself clinging to the rocky heights, with the Urubamba River far below on either side as it made its hairpin bend around the mountain. In front of me was the square stone I had seen in my dream.

Instinctively, I lay across the stone and tried to focus on my prayers, "Father, I am willing to sacrifice my life, even to the very extinction of my identity, if necessary to end this painful game of separation we have constructed. I shield my mother, the Earth, with my life and my body in any way that is needed from the hostile intentions of the misguided ones. I call upon the forces of light to surround her with protection, and I place myself here as an offering." I lay in silence and waited while the noonday sun burned brightly above.

My thoughts were jerked back to the present by a male voice speaking in a foreign tongue, coming from a position where nobody could have been standing. I turned my head slightly but couldn't see anyone. I continued to wait. The unmistakable smell of a breath laced with coca leaves blew into my face, yet still, no one appeared. As I squinted in the bright sunlight, an outline became visible. I could see the image of an Inca priest with a breastplate of gold and a tall feathered headdress. He raised his hands upward and it seemed as though he pulled something out of the sun. The next second a crystal shaft that looked liked a stalactite plunged downward and entered my breast. A sharp pain ripped through my chest and I blacked out. Two hours later when I regained consciousness, I made my way back, with wobbly knees and an aching chest, to Larry and Farrah.

I felt completely different, as though I were nothing and everything all at once. All labels to describe myself seemed ridiculously inappropriate. I felt as naked as a newly shorn lamb, devoid of all petty self-importance. I had an overwhelming urge to sleep that lasted for two days. My head lolled around like a rag doll in the trains, vans, and planes as we made our way back to Oregon.

My reunion with Brent was moving. I had focused so much on the moment that I hadn't realized how much I had missed the sight of his dear face until the airplane brought me closer and closer. I shared with him how strongly I had felt his presence while on the mountain. He had burned candles for me in our healing chamber all that day, and had mingled his own prayers with ours. I had always been linked to him in a telepathic way that couldn't be described, but our connection seemed to deepen.

The Journey Begins

Within a month of the Peruvian trip, I found myself completely overwhelmed. My phone started ringing at six in the morning and continued until late at night. I was inundated with people seeking healings. People would drive from as far as Denver, claiming to be "in the area." I would collect Brent from school, only to return and find people sobbing on the doorstep. There were times when we turned the car around and drove to the beach, seeking privacy. My friend, Amy, would come over and help by answering stacks of letters.

Then one day, my mind entirely disconnected. I thought I was having a breakdown of some sort. I couldn't remember how to pick up a pen. I couldn't remember my own phone number. As soon as I stopped fighting this, however, the effortless knowing that flows from Godmind took over. Without thinking, I could accomplish many hours of work in one hour. All flowed effortlessly.

The overwhelming neediness of the people continued, and I cried to God for help, "Father, I'm tired. I need time off. I need a life. Even the weekends would do."

As I listened for the answer, I heard someone laughing, "You are now to go out on the road and teach."

"But I don't want to teach!" I exclaimed.

Then came the reply, "It is when you no longer want to teach that you are ready."

I mulled this over in my head, rationalizing that no one connected with the lecture circuit knew about me. I was tucked away in this small town on the West Coast, and most likely, public lectures would develop gradually.

I was mistaken. Within two weeks I would be speaking in front of a large audience. The instruction came, "Go to Santa Fe." I was puzzled since I knew of nothing that was taking place in Santa Fe. A few hours later my Lakota friend called and said, "Almine, you should be in Santa Fe. There is a Star Visions Conference taking place there." The next morning my friend, Mary Beth, called and said that she was going to Santa Fe, and asked if I would like to accompany her. I cleared my calendar and called up to register as a student. As I spoke to Anthony, who organized this event, his crown chakra started opening and he felt dizzy and light. I also called him the next day, and again this profound experience, as well as an opening in his heart, occurred. He said, "Almine, I don't think you're supposed to register as a student; you're supposed to speak here."

I faxed him a poorly written description of what I thought I did and an even more vague description of what I thought I would be talking about. Even as I tried to describe it, I heard loudly and clearly, "I shall tell you what to speak and the words will come from Me." I asked God how I would be able to make the people see those marvelous insights that I had experienced, since they were beyond description. I had spent so many hours accessing the hidden realms on behalf of clients that the unseen realms had become more real to me than the seen ones.

The following three nights, I dreamt that I felt a slight knocking on my heart. As I looked down at my chest, my heart opened wider and wider—exposing the moon and the sun and the stars of our solar system. It opened beyond the speed of light, further and further, until it enclosed the whole galaxy. Eventually many galaxies became visible through my expanded heart. Finally I could see that galaxies were just pinpricks of light in the spiraling arms that swirled out from the central sun of our universe. This expansion didn't stop until all creation was contained within me. The voice spoke, "This is who you are, a consciousness superimposed over All That Is." When this dream repeated itself a third night in a row, I realized that this was a meditation that I was to share with others.

Following that, I started dreaming of a large crystal about two feet long. After several nights of seeing the crystal in my dreams, I found a yearning tugging at my heart during the day, almost as though I were in love. When I stopped to see where this tugging came from, I realized that it was the crystal in my dreams. I called the local crystal shops, asking if they had a crystal of that size, but to no avail. As I drove to the airport on the way to Santa Fe, the voice of the crystal was unmistakable. I turned my car around to where I had heard it, walked into a shop and saw the huge, two-foot crystal of my dreams.

I was astounded by the price and asked the shop owner if she could possibly make it a bit more affordable. She willingly obliged. (I later heard that the shop owner felt as though she were in an altered state when she reduced the price down to nearly cost and wondered if I had "bewitched" her!)

Once in New Mexico, I had some free time prior to my lecture. I had been working so hard that every free moment assumed a blissful importance, much like food tastes after a prolonged fast. I reveled in the soft, glorious tones of light that danced on the beautiful, yet austere, landscape.

That weekend at the Glorietta Center near Santa Fe changed my life forever. It was my first time speaking in front of a large group of people about the mystical secrets of my life. I had been instructed by Spirit not to prepare my speech, that sacred information would flow through me. At the end of my hour-long talk, many were openly sobbing. Some of the audience experienced spontaneous releases of Kundalini energy up their spines. (Mother Theresa described this as "a silver bullet" shooting up the spine.) I was in an altered state and had difficulty dealing with practical decisions. It hardly felt as though my feet were touching the ground, and I noticed that my eyes were seeing colors differently. Many commented on the strange glow of my skin.

At the end of my talk, I innocently suggested that if a few of the people needed healing that they could see me after class. The entire hall of people followed me outside, and I found myself unable to cope with the overwhelming situation. A beloved man named Jay, who would receive a life-altering healing that weekend (he went on to become a wonderful mystic, healer, and teacher) helped organize the people into groups. The organizers of the event were understandably perturbed at the absence of an audience for the next speaker, but they made a room available for the first group to come for healing.

I prayed silently, "Father, I usually take an hour for each person, how will I work with the hundreds of people this weekend?" The reply came, "I will strengthen and quicken you and you shall be My servant. You will do in a few moments what took hours before. Healing will pour through your eyes and your voice and your hands as you bind up their wounds and cause the lame to walk." I started healing the many that came, and my tears and theirs flowed freely for the next three days.

I held each one's face in my hands and gazed deeply into their eyes, acknowledging their divinity. I wondered how the energy blocks within them could release merely by the gaze of my eyes. Then suddenly I saw before me the face of Mother Meera, and realized that this was exactly what she did with the multitudes that came to her to be healed.

The energy that flowed was so powerful that at times it shook my body as I stood with my hands on someone's head. I had felt people's feelings very strongly before, but this weekend it was as though their pain was mine, and at times the intensity of it racked my body. I remember having my hands on a young woman's head and pausing a minute trying to recognize the spirit Being standing next to her. I also sensed an animal by her feet. Suddenly, she started laughing uncontrollably. She tried to stifle it, but I encouraged her to allow it. When she almost collapsed from the laughter that was rippling through her, I informed her, "The presence next to you is that of Ama Terasu, goddess of childlike play and innocence. The animal at your feet is a little monkey, which is the Mayan symbol for innocence and play." As I got ready to proceed with her blessing, I found, to my amazement, that her energy blockages had been released during those moments of laughter.

As I came to the end of the healing sessions that first day, a woman sat with tears streaming across her beautiful face. Her name was Mary Lou, and as I walked up to her, it felt as though I had known her for eons—as though she were part of my soul. I asked her to stand and simply held her in my arms and asked, "Father, through the love of my heart for this beautiful woman, I take all her pain." Immediately, my cells seemed to go into shock. (In the future, I only used that technique when specifically instructed by Spirit.) I shook uncontrollably with waves of pain rolling through my body, and staggered to the side of the room. The experience of negativity in my cells had become unfamiliar.

It amazed me that I could take on another's suffering. I turned to prayer and was gently reprimanded by Spirit, "You must not become encumbered by the weight of self reflection. You must not relate to these experiences, for in doing so, you obstruct these energies from moving through you so they can be transmuted."

That night I started burning with fever. It felt as though a furnace had been lit inside, yet I felt chilled to the bone. I lay there shaking beneath the blankets. I was told by the soft whispers of Spirit that this was burning away the negativity and density that I had absorbed from those I had blessed that day.

The next day, a Native American, who had been silently observing the healings, came forward with a bowl of smudge and fanned it around the room and onto me to assist in removing any accumulated dense energy that had resulted from the healings. He was one of the last who came to me for a healing. As he spoke about a few physical symptoms, I said to him, "But what about the devastating event that happened when you were five-and-a-half? Some of your soul pieces left during this trauma and must be brought back this day." He started crying. He told me about the trauma of that past event. I asked him whether he was ready to bring the soul pieces back that had left, explaining that these soul pieces, when returned, must be expressed or they would leave again. Tears still shook his shoulders as he promised himself that they would be allowed to fully express.

As I did the soul retrieval, I felt the presence of an old man come in from the North. "Your grandfather is here," I said. The healing was profound, and he was unable to move for at least 30 minutes as the emotional release had shaken him to his core. He explained that this grandfather, who had died long ago, had raised him. In times of trouble or triumph he always felt his presence. This man would later join me in many lectures to share the Native American spirituality with my classes.

As I worked on clients that weekend, the soft, gentle calling of the crystal, which was now in the trunk of my car at the Portland airport, continued to linger in the back of my head like a melody. (When I returned and finally placed this large crystal in my healing chamber, the room filled with angels.)

Another man, who couldn't receive a healing that weekend due to time restraints, flew to my home in Oregon. He had a large tear in his etheric body. I asked what electrical trauma he had received, and he explained that as a teenager he had undergone shock treatments, ordered by his parents. I also found an object resembling a ritualistic knife or dagger stuck into his body, and although unnoticeable to the physical eye, it was causing him great distress. When I described it to him, he said that this was an object that he had bought while in Central America. This became an important lesson because I realized that so-called "power objects" may have been negatively programmed by those of the undeveloped light. That negative energy remains with the object as it passes from one owner to another.

An Abundance of Miracles

A Message on the Wind–Many letters poured in when I returned home and I became so overwhelmed that I hired a manager, simply trusting that somehow the venues would pay his salary. One day I stood in my garden with the wind blowing through my hair and I heard, "Go to the stack of letters. At the bottom is a green envelope. Call that woman." I easily found the little green envelope from a woman named Sally. There was a small check inside. It was what she could afford, she said. She wanted in some way to express her gratitude since she had gone to many health practitioners from the East and West to help heal an injury to her shoulder from a car accident. All of her attempts had been in vain until I laid my hand upon her shoulder in a loving gesture, when she came to ask me a question. She said that all pain was now gone and that she wanted me to come to Orcas Island to teach. She had given her phone number and I called her immediately. Sally broke out crying, "Just minutes ago I stood upon the cliff overlooking the ocean and asked the wind to take you this message. You had said in your talk that the wind was your friend." Not long after, my manager organized the workshop on Orcas Island, and although the attendance was small, the feeling was powerful. I gave several more lectures at Orcas Island over the years and the group of friends became like family.

Column of Light–It was at Orcas Island that I noticed an abrupt change in the way the healing energies flowed through me. Whereas, previously it had issued forth from the pineal gland in the center of my head and out through my hands, it now felt as though a column of light was descending over me. While in this light I could distinctly feel the presence of the Christ. A man named Neil, who had received a transformational blessing in New Mexico, had decided to devote many months of his life to assisting me as I traveled on the road. He did this in faithful service without any compensation, because he wanted others to experience the same joyous changes. It was Neil who saw the image of the Master appear above my head and slowly descend to fill the place where I was standing.

A Natural Bypass–Over the next few months I made many wonderful and enduring friendships, including Tom and Theresa. Theresa was one of the first to levitate above the healing table as I worked on her. However, it was through Tom that a truly remarkable miracle occurred. Tom had experienced a heart attack that had put him in intensive care about 10 days before he came for a healing. Tests revealed that Tom hadn't recovered yet.

As usual, I took the time to explain to Tom why he had created this, noting that the narrowing of the primary arteries of the heart usually corresponded with love withheld or denied in primary relationships. I understood from looking at his life that because of unreturned love from his daughter, Tom had been trying hard not to love her as deeply as he had. The true challenge of relationships is to learn to love without pain. After exploring ways that Tom could love her without expecting anything in return, I did the healing. It felt complete and I thanked God for the gift of his healing.

I was in the Denver area when I received a distressed call on the etheric levels from his wife. I called to see what was the matter and found that Tom had experienced a massive heart attack and had been admitted to the hospital. When I went to see him, I was very puzzled. I had felt completion and peace after his healing, so how could this have happened?

While in the hospital room, it was explained to me: Tom, indeed, had had a massive heart attack but somehow in the 10 days since the previous angiogram, a large arterial bypass had formed, as though bypass surgery had been done. The bypass led precisely around the clot that had produced the heart attack, and without it, the doctors assured him he would have died. The doctor further stated that a major artery simply didn't form such a bypass voluntarily, especially in such a short period of time. (Natural bypasses do occur in the small veins of the body but even those require more time.) Hence, the healing I had given had created the large arterial bypass.

Stilling the Storm–I found that the etheric communication with those who attended my lectures was increasing. Once, when I came to a new venue, I asked the audience how many had seen me either in visions, dreams, or meditations prior to that day. Over half raised their hands. It seemed that at higher levels I was being sent to gather together those whom I would eventually teach. At first when students would silently call me for assistance, I would briefly see their face flash before me. Later, as I became more accustomed to this unique method of communication, I would become aware that a piece of me was leaving to respond to their call. A beautiful Native American woman, Cindy, was on a vision quest with four days of fasting and prayer when a cold front settled in and rain drenched the inadequate blanket that she had taken. As she called upon me for assistance, an opening occurred directly above her in the dark stormy clouds and a shaft of sunlight shone down and warmed her in her Medicine Circle where she was praying. All around her the storm continued.

Shekinah Melchizedek and the Initiation of Gethsemane

Brent has always been an empath. At times it has been a burden to carry. For instance, at the age of 12, just passing by the shoes of the other kids at school would cause him to feel the heartaches and griefs, the joys and the triumphs of each owner's life.

It was during the summer that he received a vision of an iron rod with a banner at the top displaying a sacred symbol. As he called me from England to try and describe his vision, I could instantly see what he had seen. It was in September that I was told to prepare this rod for him, and that it was to be ready on the autumnal equinox. I covered the metal rod in soft white leather and made the banner from white leather with gold lettering. From this, I hung two swan feathers that were gathered from the retreat where Yogananda had lived. The image of the swan was very strong around Brent, as is common with masters of light.

When the fall equinox arrived, the Universe had prepared many auspicious visitors to bless the day. With one hour's notice, I was told that 12 Tibetan Buddhist monks would be coming for lunch. I hastily prepared a large buffet and was ready by the time their friendly brown faces came through the door. They asked if they could chant for us, and I took them up to the healing chamber. Even after they left, their song continued to reverberate through our house for about two hours.

Later, I was given instructions to do an initiation on Brent at a specific time. I was told to surround him with rose quartz and roses at his feet. I went into prayer to prepare for this event and I received his sacred name. At first I couldn't properly hear the first word. After three faltering attempts on my part to say it correctly, it was as though someone shouted in my ear, "She-ki-nah, his name is Shekinah Melchizedek." As I initiated him that day, a female Being of great light appeared before me and said, "You have done well. You may hand him over now." I wasn't sure what this meant, but thought that he may be leaving life at this time. I started crying, reluctant to part with him. Then another Being appeared, a higher aspect of him that said, "Mother, for this came I into the world." I did the dedication and Brent received the message that he was to get up at a specific time that night to do a ceremony for the Earth. I set the alarm but I didn't sleep much. The lead monk who had been in my home earlier that day, appeared to me out-of-body, and we exchanged knowledge for two hours. He had barely left when the alarm prompted me to wake Brent. The experience my son had that night, in which he saw the Master Christ face to face, was too sacred to even discuss. For days following, he kept to himself in silence, integrating the holiness of it. A state of mastery existed in his life. The transformation was incredible, and he began to assist me in healing sessions, exerting little effort, and seeming to heal through his intense love.

His academic brilliance was such that school was hardly any effort at all, and even national exams were taken in stride. My soul seemed completely at peace when I was with him, and throughout his high school years I spent every moment I could with him.

These moments became fewer and fewer. At a higher level I could see that the grand purpose of this was to prepare him for our coming separation after high school. However, at a physical level I felt agony over his impending departure for college. During 1998 he graduated as one of the most brilliant students ever from Lincoln County, and left to do an internship in Washington, D.C.

I understood that with the path of Mastery, the student comes to what could be called the initiation of Gethsemane. It is a time when all who love us turn away and we are left to test our beliefs on our own. The following July was such a month for me. Brent joined me in South Africa for a visit to the San Bushmen and a safari in the Urusaba Game Reserve. His hostility was unmistakable. I was baffled by this unaccustomed emotion from him. I didn't know what to do, therefore, I did nothing. I knew that in the life of every student there comes a time when one finds fault with the teacher so that he or she may cut the "umbilical" cord. I had thought since we were more than teacher and student that such a thing wouldn't occur in Brent's life. I was wrong.

I knew it was necessary for him to immerse himself in the physical world for his entry into Stanford University. To accomplish that, he also needed to develop an emotional detachment from me. He firmly established this by rejecting everything that I stood for, including blocking out the memory of the miracles that he had witnessed.

I had heard of people who wanted to leave but couldn't due to obligations, and therefore received a "Walk-In" spirit to take their place, while they left for the Spirit world. I briefly wondered if this had occurred to Brent since not even his tastes in art or food were the same. I later understood that this was simply one more attempt to break the attachment to what he felt I represented.

One afternoon he verbally attacked virtually everything that I was living and had taught him. He demanded that I provide a miracle if I were able. I said very little but reeled under the onslaught. I searched my inner wisdom, questioning whether or not I should demonstrate something miraculous to change his mind.

I deduced since the miracles he had seen before didn't impress him, that nothing else would either. I was reminded that the Pharisees discarded the miracles that Christ had done. These popular lyrics came into my head, "A man hears what he wants to hear and disregards the rest." From a personal standpoint, I knew that I would be reduced from a Mystic walking a path of impeccability to a mere Sorcerer by doing a miracle just to persuade someone.

Brent left for college convinced that his mother was delusional.

Within two weeks, Almine Jr. and her former husband, Jason, delivered the second verbal attack. They grabbed at every conceivable thing that I might possibly have done that was "dishonoring" to them, disregarding the $9,000 that I had just spent on their wedding. I tried to listen behind the words to what was really going on, and I found a similar motive to Brent's, for Almine and Jason had also been living in my shadow. For a while Jason had even managed my office. They were tired of the multitudes of people who were using them to get some of my time. They had become resentful. They decided to move to Hawaii to get as far away from me as they could. Almine Jr. thought that there she could be a woman in her own right and not just my daughter. She asked if she could call me by my first name. I said that she could call me what she wished—that my love for her would remain steadfast.

Later that same month, many of my students turned away due to a slanderous assault on my character by a vindictive couple. I had become tired so I went to the desert to pray with Donya, my secretary at that time. The solitude there helped me put things into perspective. It was like balm to my soul.

In 1998 and 1999 there was a gradual softening towards me from both Almine Jr. and Brent. Almine Jr. had gone through some very hard knocks and had begun to realize that the one person in the world whom she could count on was her mother. She decided that having a mother wasn't so bad after all and even began calling me Mother again.

This was the first time in my life I had no one to come home to. The aching for my son became a constant gnawing pain. I kept myself distracted by plunging headlong into my work. I went on many extended tours, traveling wherever there were willing hearts that wanted to listen. Seven day seminars for groups of men or women were arranged at my home, and extraordinary miracles occurred. Twice the men's groups managed to achieve such a heightened state of awareness that I levitated before them. Angels, clearly visible to the majority, were ministering to them. During one such occasion, I was taken out-of-body and found myself standing above the world, observing as it rotated with its cloudy veils. Jesus the Christ, stood beside me and told me of the rare and incredible future of this beloved planet and how it would become the pivotal point that starts all of existence on the road home to the Heart of God. Much was revealed to me that I wouldn't be given permission to teach until 2001.

During this year I led a tour to Peru, and the trip to Lake Titicaca turned out to be a harrowing experience for me. The closer we came to the lake, the more my anxiety grew. By the time we checked into our hotel on the edge of the lake, I was hyperventilating. I went into a past memory of my crashing into this lake, and my lungs filling with icy cold water. The experience was so real that it felt as though my reason was coming apart at the seams, and I could hardly remember where I was. My mouth had turned completely blue, and they had to send for oxygen.

The terror went through me in waves, and I realized that it stemmed from my plunging into a density to which I was entirely unaccustomed. I had known that great trauma was attached to my birth, as my breath was fragmented and not deep, and it had been that way all of my life. Spirit had told me that this was due to the terror I felt coming into this density from a higher vibrational life. I struggled for breath as women helped me through the night. I dared not sleep for I would immediately stop breathing. Memories of similar occurrences in early childhood were strongly present. I remembered gasping for breathe and turning blue long ago, just as I was doing then. I left the group and Lake Titicaca the next morning with Brent and a beloved assistant, Debbie. Thereafter, I noticed much of the terror held within had been released, as my breathing was deeper and less fragmented. I emerged from this experience feeling much lighter than before.

The Mother of All Languages

Towards the end of 1999, I was in prayer when it occurred to me to ask the great Master, Thoth, for an object that had belonged to him. The next morning a one-inch scarab materialized in front of my bed. I cautiously examined it, without touching it, for several days. Did Thoth really leave this for me? Finally, I decided to claim this sacred item and picked it up. I went outside and kneeled on the lawn, preparing for a prayer of thanks. At that moment, a flock of unusual finches settled around me in the garden. I had never seen these before. I counted the birds in one bush and there were over 100. Every bush and tree had filled with birds so they must have totaled at least a 1,000! They seemed unafraid of me and sang their songs with almost deafening exuberance. "Thank you Thoth, I accept this gift with gratitude," I said. And on the last word, as though someone had held up a baton, the little birds flew into the sky and disappeared. Since that incident, I have never seen this type of bird on the Oregon coast.

From the moment those birds disappeared, a strange language started forming in the recesses of my mind and soon the pressure to speak it became stronger and stronger until it gushed forth. As the language flowed and flowed, I could hear the telepathic translation within my mind. I noticed that it had sounds that I had never heard before in any of the languages I spoke, and some of the letters such as "R" or "P" were missing. When I inquired where this language had come from, it said that this was the "mother of all languages" spoken upon our planet. I found that speaking this language in my classes awakened the memory of ancient languages in other people.

One particular workshop held in Elora, Ontario, activated so many peoples' memories, that by the end of the week over half the class of 45 students were either speaking or writing the ancient symbols. In March of 2000, I started to write the vertical formation of glyphs of the language I spoke, and I asked that it be placed on my web site. One month later, "Popular Science" magazine produced a photograph of eight glyphs, five of which were identical to the ones I had placed on our web site the month before. They said that this had been discovered in Southern Egypt and that it substantially pushed back the date historians usually associated with the Egyptian culture. It was a delight to me when I discovered that a dear friend, Andrew, in England, spoke the same language and we have had great joy speaking it together.

I returned to Denver after a few years of absence and was delighted to see my friends who felt like family members. After class, as was my custom, I asked them to turn the lights down for those who wanted to stay for blessings. As I placed my hands upon the head of one woman, I could feel that something was definitely not as it seemed. I knelt down in front of her and looked at her beautiful face. Yes, I remembered her. She had come to me before and spoke about wanting to leave her life but was unable to because of her daughter and her husband. The face was the same, but the vibration I felt was completely different. I asked her to wait until I had completed all the healings and then come with me to my hotel room so that I could spend an hour with her.

During the hour she told me the following story: Since our last meeting, she had been in a severe car crash. A truck struck a car she was a passenger in and it became airborne. She remembered the feeling of dying and leaving her body. She also remembered holding onto a door handle to be able to re-enter the body. (Later when she examined the crumbled vehicle, there was no handle.) When she returned home from the hospital she went to her bedroom and everything felt strange and new, as though she had never seen it before. She awoke the next day and looked through her window and saw a neighbor shoot his pig with a gun. The pig squealed in agony and he kept shooting bullets into its head. She slipped into a state of shock and remained that way for several days. Since then she had hardly wanted to leave her room. All her friends had fallen by the wayside. The only activities she participated in were with her husband and child, yet even those activities didn't seem to fit.

I went into deep prayer to find some answers for her. I could clearly see that the woman that had inhabited this body had left for the Spirit World, as she had wanted to, and that a higher Being had come in to occupy the body. Such an occurrence is called a "Walk-In". The Walk-In had undertaken to fulfill all the obligations of the previous Being's life but this new personality was of a very high level of consciousness. Seeing the barbarism of the human race by the killing of a pig in such an inhumane manner had put this Being, who was new to earth, into a state of shock.

After explaining to her that she was a Walk-In, I welcomed her into the body, and gave her an initiation and blessing. I had quickened the vibration of the body so that it would be comfortable for this Being to inhabit. She held out her hand and blessed me in a language not of this earth. The full majesty and force of a God-realized being in the flesh shone through her eyes.

The Holy Transformation 1999 – 2000

On November 22, 1999, I adopted Jaylene, a 9-month-old Cree Indian girl. I had only seen her in a photograph but instantly knew that I was to be part of her life. She had been abandoned at the age of three months and then removed from the foster home that she had been placed in. She had much fear of abandonment and clung to me with her tiny fists. It melted my heart.

Needless to say, she changed my life completely. My lecturing tours were carefully planned and she accompanied me on the longer trips so that she wouldn't feel abandoned again.

A month later I was baffled by strange symptoms in my body. At night it would feel as though my heart stopped, and at times, so would my breath. I could feel presences around my bed as soon as I placed my head on the pillow. I frequently awoke drenched at night but somehow the wetness of my body didn't resemble sweat. In fact, it wasn't salty, and had a more viscous consistency. In the morning, huge black and blue bruises would be visible over the major acupuncture points of my body, only to disappear within an hour. I had become unbearably fatigued and the slightest exertion would cause my heart to pound.

Traveling with a toddler from country to country was an extreme hardship, and I wished that I had some sort of support system, such as extended family or close relatives to help. Monique did what she could yet she lived 150 miles away so there was limited access. Some nights the physical symptoms were so severe that I wondered if I was dying, and on two occasions, I checked myself into the emergency room. The hospital tests showed that my systemic functions were normal. I took the matter to Spirit and was told that it would end in September of the following year, when I would merge with an angel.

I was puzzled by these words. Weren't angels an entirely different line of evolution? How could I possibly merge with an angel? Did I even want to? Human life was precious and I had often urged my students not to let guides or any other Beings control them. Though confused, I surrendered myself into God's hands and counted the days until September. Most of September came and went and a group of men came to my house for a vision quest during the last week. I took them to a cave to spend three days and nights fasting and in prayer. I returned home with Jaylene.

That night after putting her to bed, something took place that took me months to fully comprehend. It felt as though a fire had ignited within my spine and energy shot through my body. I looked in the mirror, and for a moment couldn't see my face because of the light that was shining out of it. Even looking down at my hands and arms was a strange experience. White light radiated through my skin more abundantly than ever before and a violet flame had formed upon my head. I was reminded of the experience at Pentecost when flames appeared on the heads of those present. A sphere of light had appeared above my head approximately the size of a large salad plate. In the next instant, energy bursts occurred in the middle of my shoulder blades and two large wings of light shot out behind me. As I continued staring into the mirror that forms one wall of my bedroom, a "skirt" of light also radiated downward and I heard the words, "The stone, remember the stone".

I went over to my altar and picked up a stone that had come to me in a miraculous way from the Master Sanat Kumara. In fact, it wasn't a stone at all but a fossilized bone that fit comfortably into the palm. On one side of its surface was carved the dove in a circle. As Yogananda had said, this was the symbol for the sacred fire that ignites when the masculine and the feminine energies combine. The shape of the dove with its beak pointing upward, the wings out-stretched, and the tail fanned at the bottom, was an approximation of the energy field that had formed around my body. The beak pointing upward was like the flame on my head. The wings represented the wings of light that had burst out of my shoulder blades, and a pyramid of light radiated down towards the ground from the position of my ovaries. I knew, in that moment, that all 12 chakras had opened, and that at some point, the sphere above my head would encompass all of the other chakras just as depicted on the stone. I could continue to see this amazing energy configuration around my body for several hours before it faded from my vision. Everything felt different and from that day forth, the uncomfortable physical symptoms disappeared.

Over the next month, I felt almost detached from my experiences. I walked around in a daze. I noticed that I could more clearly perceive energy. My perception of time was completely altered. The past seemed as accessible as the future, as though I were in the middle of a spiderweb and time lay in all directions. I could see all probable futures at once and it became very difficult to make decisions. My staff struggled with me as I could hardly make my usual decisions about future plans. It felt as though there were no future. I decided that it was time to write my life's story. I had the uncanny feeling that I was establishing a permanent record that led up to something unforeseeable. I felt as I did during the days preceding the birth of my children. It was as though some life-altering event was about to be birthed, and that I had to recall the events that led up to it. I feverishly dictated the story of my life, driven by an urgency I couldn't comprehend.

During the days of October, I worked late into each night ensuring that no details were forgotten. During the first week of November, I began to experience increased ecstatic states. The walls of my house were sometimes visible and sometimes not. Speaking had become almost redundant. Everyone's intentions seemed crystal clear to me and their words were heard before they were formed.

I left on the first Friday of November for Dallas/Ft. Worth, Texas, to teach a group of novices that had become familiar with my work through a beloved friend, Karolynn. She took me to her massage therapy office and as she started working on me, the sacred words of the "I AM" channeled through her. I became so expanded that I could hardly walk. Later that evening, as I gave my introductory talk, the Archangel Michael entered the class and channeled through me. He called himself Mi-ka-el and told the class members to ask for what they wanted and they would receive it. Many of them asked for expanded vision, to be able to see into the hidden realms, and because of this request they were able to see the great Masters of Light during the following two days as events unfolded.

At the end of the Friday night session, one woman was crying uncontrollably and relayed the following story: As she had set up the room in preparation for the event, she had been promised help from a few staff members of the hotel. Although they never came, a young man appeared and looked around as though he hadn't been there before. He said that he had come to help. His behavior was strange to her. He simply didn't seem like a hotel staff member and when he walked over to the table where she had displayed my tapes, he said, "She looks like an angel. This is going to be a very special event and they will need special water." He removed the tap water that had been set out in pitchers and came back with other water saying, "This is special water for such a special event." After helping her set up the chairs he turned at the door and said over his shoulder, "Tell her my name is Mi-ka-el."

The next day the Master, Jesus the Christ, appeared next to me, visible to many in class, and then moved into the space where I stood. I started to speak the words that I could hear within my head as He gave the prophecy, "Upon the backs of a few the future will pivot and great are the events of this holy day."

In the blink of an eye I lost all identity and disconnected from ego or body identification. I saw the Infinite within me. I saw the central suns of the universes joined by a beam of light through my heart, like a strand of pearls. At that moment I knew without a doubt that "I AM the I AM", meaning I am both the creation and the creator—the beginning and the end.

I was instructed not to let anyone touch me during that holy Saturday. During the lunch hour, while in my room I levitated above the floor and with the assistance of Karolynn, I became grounded enough to return to class. She helped me speak to the students since words weren't coming easily. My awareness had expanded to include all of creation and it seemed like a super-human task to walk or speak.

Any food or water sent me into a state of ecstasy. That night as I sat down to eat my dinner, a bite of salmon catapulted me into the entire life scenario of the fish I was eating. I saw him enthusiastically make his way down the river to the ocean. I felt the sting-ing of the salt in his gills for the first few days. I saw him rise to the surface of the ocean and through his eyes the sunset appeared yellowish-gold. I felt his fear as he struggled in the net and gasped his final breaths. Similarly I experienced the life of the grain and vegetables upon my plate.

The following day the experience continued. I felt myself observing my body from afar and at times I couldn't find it at all. In my lunch hour, when left alone, I felt as though I might vibrate out of this reality all together. It was a struggle to stay in the physi-cal body. By the end of that day I embraced every one of the class members and tears just flowed. The holiness was so powerful there were no words for our feelings. By the evening when I left for the airport I wandered as though in a daze and had great difficulty being self-aware enough to become oriented to my environment.

Channelings came through Karolynn during the coming days to give me instructions as to how to handle the God-realization into which I had been catapulted. Even language that was separation-based no longer fit into my comprehension. I was instructed to eat only that which "lives," for energies would be entering my body that weren't from this universe. I did as instructed but the words were meaningless to me, as all universes existed within me. Ecstatic states continued to be produced by the intake of any food or water.

An indescribable compassion poured forth from me that embraced every creature. Life was forever altered for me. I mir-rored the words from the Odes of Solomon, "Nothing appeared closed to me because I was the door of everything."

PART TWO

Mystical Keys
to Ascension

CHAPTER TWO

GOD'S GRAND DESIGN

Your Identity in God's Design

The greatest secret ever kept is the identity of man: a being as vast as the cosmos, having a human experience. We are powerful, creator Gods who have come from every corner of the galaxy to be on earth at this crucial time when mankind and the earth are ascending into a new energetic frequency. We are in the process of moving from an era of dark materialism that resulted in separation consciousness, into a group-minded era of compassion and heightened awareness.

Your role in this is extraordinary, for you already have the answers to the seeming woes of this planet. You have arrived to bring the solutions on how to assist humanity and the earth during this transition.

The majority of you are star-born. I received the revelation that those whom this message would reach are the sons and daughters of light whom the prophets have been anticipating for thousands of years. You have come to live with one foot on earth and one foot in the higher realms to bridge the energies and make the shift as smooth as possible. You are a living bridge of light.

God created all beings perfectly. He created us as heirs to His kingdom with the ability to create through thought and feeling. We are so powerful that we created the earth exactly as she is now. We did this innocently of course, not realizing that all that the Father has is ours, thus, there is no need for competition or hoarding. It appears we have created suffering and destruction, and we have, but there would be no growth without resistance.

There would be no evolution of God's awareness if we came to earth remembering that we are already one with God. God's awareness evolves through our experiences, therefore, we had to incarnate in a state of forgetfulness to experience growth. We had to set up a game pretending to be separate from others and separate from God. We also had to pretend there are places where God is not. This is an effective learning technique because sometimes it takes experiencing who we are not, in order to understand more fully who we are. For this game to work, we needed polarity. That is why one-third of the host of heaven agreed to be light retarders. One-third agreed to be light promoters, or Lightworkers. And one-third agreed to observe and learn the lessons.

How effortlessly this ascension takes place depends on the diligence with which the Lightworkers are preparing themselves. The larger the number of people who ascend prior to the earth moving to a higher dimension, the more smoothly the transition takes place.

How can one Lightworker make a difference? It happens when we take the unknown possibilities that could occur in our life and incorporate them into known reality through experience. Through this, we are allowing God to experience what had been unknown. Hence, we assist in evolving God's awareness in the most astonishing way. That is how important each life is!

Imagine the universe as a huge, intricate spiderweb. Every person and being constitutes a thread. If one were to pull out even a single thread, it would be broken. Most people feel insignificant picturing themselves as only one tiny thread of the billions that comprise the gigantic, universal spiderweb. However, when they see the big picture, they realize they are the potential means by which God can experience trillions of possibilities. As we unfold the mysteries of the unknown parts of our lives, God's library of known experiences increases.

The known is merely accessed light, meaning it has already been experienced. The unknown is light that isn't accessed or experienced yet; it is undeveloped light. We regard the dark, undeveloped light as evil, but it is simply the unknown parts of the Infinite waiting to be explored. This is accomplished by embracing the challenges that come our way. When we gain insights from these challenges, the undeveloped light, which wasn't experienced up to this point, becomes accessible or known. Thus, as we include the dark within the light, there is more light. Light is information, consequently, our reward is increased knowledge.

This great secret of our true identity has caused the greatest battle on this planet: to have control over the minds of men. The last thing the light retarders want us to know is how powerful we are. If we realized that all power lies within us and we need nothing from anyone, they would lose all control over us. Therefore, they have worked hard to hide this truth. This is accomplished mostly through generating fear and suppression of the things that would set men free, such as the intuitive and the spiritual.

The way to combat this onslaught is to become uncontrollable. We do so by freeing ourselves from rational fears and rational expectations and remembering who we are.

When we fully grasp this, we know we are not the atom—we are the whole. We are the One expressing as the many and with our destruction, the whole universe will fall.

What is Ascension?

Ascension is defined in Webster's dictionary as rising to a higher level or degree. For our purposes of discussion, this pertains to mankind's and the earth's consciousness that is unfolding to a higher level. Consciousness is measured by how many levels of awareness we can access at once.

The nucleus of each cell is a bridge to the presence of the Divine. At a physical level, our consciousness rises to the highest degree possible when our cells become filled with light. If we live our life through unconditional love, it causes the nucleus to expand and fill the whole cell. Some scriptures refer to this as becoming spiritualized. This is ascension and it results in a quickening of our overall vibrational rate, hence, allowing us to more fully contain the Spirit of God.

Moving up to the Fourth Dimension

Where are we going when we ascend?

If we ascend as an individual prior to the mass ascension of humanity, we move from the third dimension to the upper sixth dimension. We join the White Brotherhood, those of all races and all religions, who have overcome all things while in the flesh. As an ascended master, we can travel at will from the sixth dimension throughout the lower realms.

Those who ascend during the mass ascension with the earth, will move up to the fourth dimension. However, if a full ascension occurs, it will have to be a movement into the sixth dimension. The earth may not initially make a full ascension, probably moving to the fourth dimension first, then making a further ascension up to the sixth dimension.   12 levels in 12 dimen·

The ascension may happen gradually—overtone[1] by overtone—meaning we may not notice that we have moved into the fourth dimension.

The majority of people will move into the higher dimension without dying. The Lightworkers, due to their increased vibration, will energetically carry millions with them. Those of a lower consciousness will be able to withstand the shift since the Lightworkers are increasing the overall consciousness of the population a little bit, year-by-year. This will lessen the shock to humanity.

Some have chosen to remain unaware so a unique situation has developed on earth. The usual method of healing for a universe has been that the majority of its inhabitants remember they are one with Source and all other lifeforms. When they no longer sustain the dream of separation, it ceases and they return home. But there have been pockets of beings that still wanted to play the game of pretending to be separate. These are known as dregs. Since we have free will, they chose to remain behind. Over the millennia, the dregs increased in number and became more dense. They joined other universes, filtering down from one universe to the next. Each time the play was re-enacted in hopes they would remember their true identity, but they chose not to. Finally, they hit the bottom of the barrel—the densest of density—the lower levels of this universe. Earth has a special role as the archetype for this

1 This universe has 12 dimensions and each one has 12 levels that are called overtones.

density. Therefore, the earth has become bottom-heavy with the dregs. Some Lightworkers believe it is acceptable to leave them behind, but one cannot become whole if one cuts off a limb.

The earth exists in all dimensions at all times. This won't change. Since the earth is a sentient, living being, when a wave of humanity moves to a higher level, she becomes more conscious, meaning she will be able to access her higher dimensional aspects.

The vibrational frequency in the fourth dimension allows for whatever we think and feel to manifest instantaneously. That works well for those who are in a state of unconditional love, but our fears will instantly manifest too. That is why it is a prerequisite for us to get rid of all our fears prior to ascension.

The fourth-dimensional earth is unpolluted and our lifespans will be much longer. However, we are going to keep 2% negativity because without it, growth is slow or nonexistent. In 35 years on earth, we can grow more than the equivalent of 10,000 earth-years of life on planets inhabited only by God-realized beings. We have an incredible ability to grow due to the opposition we experience here.

What Happens to Third-Dimensional Earth?

According to our star-brothers, the third-dimensional earth will be inherited by a wave of humanity coming in from a second-dimensional planet in Sirius. If there are humans or beings who are so steeped in forgetfulness that they don't wish to move upward with the majority, they may temporarily incarnate among them. They will remain behind until they are energetically ready to join us in the higher dimensions. That fulfills the scripture that says two will be plowing, one will be taken and one will remain. We literally vibrate out of each other's sight.

It is unlikely that the third-dimensional earth will remain, as we know it now. Throughout history when civilizations have ascended, all manmade materials have dissolved and all memory of the old way of life has been erased. The new inhabitants will start over again in many ways.

Time Frame for Ascension

When is the ascension process likely to reach its peak?

The highest information I have received indicates that it will occur in the seventh month of 2013. But according to whose calendar? Lunar, solar, Mayan, or Jewish? All indications are that it is the Mayan calendar. However, it will unfold in stages, and the interface period right after the winter solstice of 2012 and into the beginning of 2013 will begin the countdown. I feel something momentous will be occurring in February 2013.

Why 2013? Many signs point to this date. The ancient prophesies of the Hopi, Egyptians and Essenes all end in the year 2013. What happens beyond that isn't known. The Hopi petroglyphs show it as a precipice that we are supposed to leap across. The calendrical systems of the world's indigenous populations—the Mayan, Aztec, I Ching, Celt, and Druid—have calendars based on 13-20.

These numbers have been put in our body and the earth. She has seven chakras on her physical surface, just as we do. We have 13 main joints and the earth has 13 main energetic plates. We have 20 fingers and toes. The planet divides into 20 sections that represent the 20 Mayan solar tribes.

Thirteen is a number that births into something new. When Jesus Christ formed the new gird around the earth, he did it with 12 disciples and himself, equaling 13.

In the mystery teachings 7, 13, 20 are the numbers for the

human minds. The subconscious mind is seven. Eight represents the left-brain and five represents the right-brain. When we add them together, they equal 13. When the left and right brains merge, we are able to continually access our Higher Self[2], which is our fourth-dimensional aspect that has designed a specific blueprint for this life in accordance with the overall mission for which we were created. Our Higher Self accesses Godmind and Godmind equates to the number 20.

More than One Way to Ascend

Ascending through feeling is the right-brain, feminine approach. This is accomplished by extending love, praise and gratitude to God, mankind and every lifeform. At that point, every act we perform becomes dedicated to the glory of God—whether it is cleaning a toilet, pumping gas into the car, or working a seemingly dull job in the county clerk's office.

Ascending through insight is the left-brain, masculine approach. It is accomplished through logic and mastery of the mind. Anything to do with self-discipline or deprivation of senses comes from left-brain ascension techniques.

These are entirely different ways of ascending, but they don't stand independently, because each enhances some components of the other. Correct perception engenders the Three Ascension Attitudes of love, praise and gratitude. These attitudes, in return, engender enhanced perception.

Unconditional love is necessary for ascension. When it exists within us, we are vibrating at the rate of God's pure intent. This vibration seeks to include. As we return to Source, we take with us

2 Higher Self represents our fourth-dimensional aspect that has designed the blueprint of this life in accordance with our overall purpose for which we were created. Our Highest Self is a consciousness superimposed over All That Is that oversees all lifetimes.

those of the undeveloped light.

The different approaches to ascension, just like different types of yoga, all get us there. Depending on our innate inclinations and abilities, one will be more appealing than another.

Within the universe, some planets are right-brain oriented so they represent the right-brain of the universe, and other planets are left-brain oriented. The earth is a right-brain planet, as indicated by the geometric fields that surround her. This means the right-brain method of ascension is more natural to humans. However, our star-brothers who were from left-brained planets have given us most of our ascension techniques. Due to that, the majority of mystery schools and major religions have accentuated left-brain techniques. This has been the case for millennia. It has only been in the last 2,000 years that the right-brain techniques have been restored.

The left-brain dominance on earth has suppressed the feminine aspects and the imbalance resulted in the earth undergoing several descensions in consciousness, which can be termed "the fall of man." After such a fall, much of the former knowledge is forgotten. Therefore, we have forgotten the natural ways for a right-brain planet to ascend. The techniques from the other planetary systems work, but it isn't natural to most humans.

Last Lifetime for Reincarnation

This is a very special time to be on earth, for it is our last lifetime in third-dimensional life as we have known it. The short reincarnational cycles end following this lifetime.

Short reincarnational cycles aren't a normal way of evolution for this planet. It has only occurred during the past 100,000 years when the light retarders used it as a means to suppress mankind. It resulted in our lifespans being dramatically shortened, from living thousands of years to approximately 76 years. We were also ensnared into losing our memory from one lifetime to the next, consequently, we became stuck in a notorious cycle of living the same scenarios over and over.

Why Ascend
Regaining Your Power

In 1997 when I first started publicly teaching, a young woman stood at the closing of the New Mexico seminar and said, "I've seen my inner power this weekend and I'll never give it away again." That sums up the entire reason why I am teaching.

Many of us have given our personal power away to our families, lovers, bosses, social structures, religious leaders and governments. We did it to obtain approval because we were taught we weren't worthy of love and that we are less than God. This is social conditioning and it is the greatest enslavement of all. By altering our perception we can break free from the limitations imposed upon us by society. Otherwise, all we need to know is how to find a job, pay taxes, and wait for death.

We must start seeing behind the appearances. Things aren't what they seem. Creation is but a reflection of a portion of the Infinite. In other words, we are living in a mirror image—a reflection of that which is real. The illusions dissolve as we bring forth our Godself.

It is time for us to reclaim our birthright of power and heal ourselves, others and the planet. We can change the course of history, but 11/12ths of power lies in the hidden realms. Those working for the undeveloped light have never forgotten this. We have. This is because we have been manipulated to be afraid of power. It is staggering how many Lightworkers have said to me, "I'm psychic, but am I supposed to know this?" The answer is always yes, because all information is available to everyone conscious enough to seize it. That is why the mystery school teachings are no longer kept secret. The information is coming forth from many sources all over the world and can be accessed within, and in some instances, outside ourselves.

When we are in balance living the ascension attitudes, we are in a state of unconditional love and we stand in the center of our personal spiderweb. Then we can expand the threads of our spiderweb to the outer-most edge of creation and all will reside within us— the planets, suns, all people and all lifeforms. At that point, we have aligned our spiderweb with the universal spiderweb and all becomes subject unto us.

We are then able to consciously travel among the dimensions, taking our physical body with us, as we choose. We can also move our consciousness into any form and freely travel throughout the cosmos. Many people experience this to some extent in the dream-state, but then it only allows us to travel within the lower astral realms. As ascended beings, we can travel throughout the 6th dimension. We may choose what we wish to experience and retain memory as we change dimensions and forms. Whether we choose to stay on earth or leave, is dependent upon what we perceive as our highest calling. And the highest calling is, "How can I best solve the unknown mysteries of being?"

However, you need not concern yourself with that question, for when you become filled with light, your Godmind comes forth and you will effortlessly know all things. Decisions won't originate from your surface mind because all answers will come from a place of inner stillness.

We will be able to master all circumstances—even the atomic elements of our body. We will multiply the loaves and fishes. Even the effects of our past wrong-doings will be erased. As our voices become awakened, we can ask that the storm be stilled and it will be. We can say, "Be thou healed," and it will happen. We will have no reason for illness or aging. When we conquer the final challenge, we also overcome death.

Signs of physical decay such as wrinkles, are the results of year-after-year of limiting attitudes and storing fear inside the body. The passage of time should have nothing to do with decay. Aging and decay are due to being a prisoner to the law of gravity. Cultivating the Three Ascension Attitudes lifts us above the law of gravity. Then our skin and muscles will reverse the aging process, even if aging has become visible.

Death is unnecessary. If we overcome it, we have rendered a huge service to mankind, for it elevates the consciousness of every man, woman and child.

There are 12 dimensions in our universe and each one has 12 overtones. When we die we go into the third and fourth overtones of the fourth dimension. In those overtones, we are still within the illusion of light and dark, as a result, we perpetuate those polarities. If we ascend, we bypass those overtones and join the White Brotherhood.

There is a River of Life that separates the middle heavens from the upper heavens. When we ascend, we pass through the barrier between the middle levels and the upper levels of earth's existence. This river is a concentrated form of love. When we pass through it, we are forever altered. That is the symbolism of baptism. If we choose to come back and live among humans, we are never the same.

When we ascend, it tears a hole in the frequency prison that surrounds the earth. This is the veil of darkness mentioned in the scriptures. Light, which cannot penetrate this electromagnetic prison directly, can be channeled through our hearts. Light channeled through a human heart is a more comfortable way for humans to experience change. If pure, white light isn't diffused through a human heart, the vibration is too strong for unaware people to hold. Hence, chaos ensues as old patterns destructure themselves.

However, if we become a plug-in for the light to radiate through the heart, we gently change people. If one is balanced and open to change, he or she will feel peace and love in our presence. If the person is imprisoned by his beliefs, he will feel irritation. That is why many prophets have been killed in the past. Although the reaction of people today isn't as antagonistic towards spiritual leaders, it never-the-less polarizes their responses and may create strong reactions.

The light on earth is increasing every year in preparation for the ascension. If the additional light is resisted, it creates havoc in some and growth in others; it is separating the wheat from the chaff.

Normally, a person has seven chakras that are conical in shape, with a plug in the center; so it looks like an hourglass when viewed from the side. The seals are formed by debris from previously unresolved issues connected with those chakras. As a person grows in consciousness, the plugs open and the cone becomes spherical and eventually spreads to form a unified chakra field. The heart of an ascended master has the seals broken within the chakras. This means his or her chakra field has become one large field.

This is the opening of the seven seals mentioned in Revelations,

Phase I of Chakra Opening

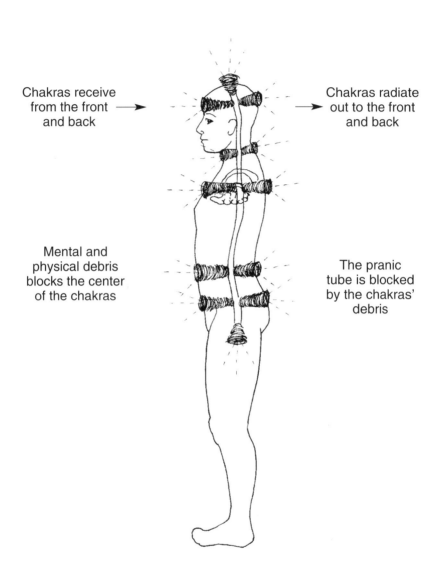

Chakras receive from the front and back →

Chakras radiate → out to the front and back

Mental and physical debris blocks the center of the chakras

The pranic tube is blocked by the chakras' debris

Seven levels of light enter the chakras. It cannot immediately assimilate and download into the endocrine system because of the blockages and acidic pH present. This occurs in the cells of a person who hasn't overcome the past and holds on to that which no longer serves him.

Phase II of Chakra Opening

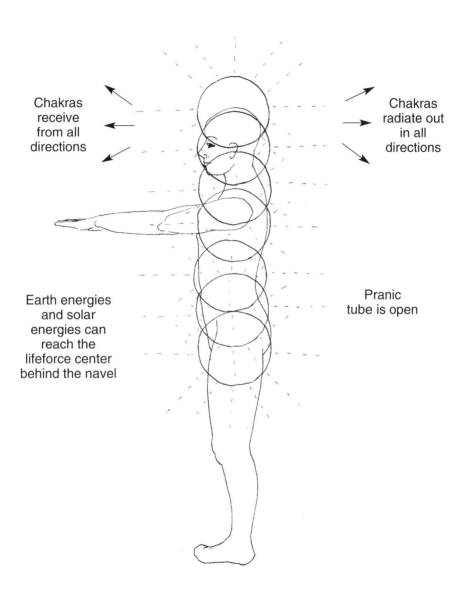

Chakras receive from all directions

Chakras radiate out in all directions

Earth energies and solar energies can reach the lifeforce center behind the navel

Pranic tube is open

Less sleep is needed while the endocrine system downloads the seven levels of light. Light is information.

Phase III of Chakra Opening

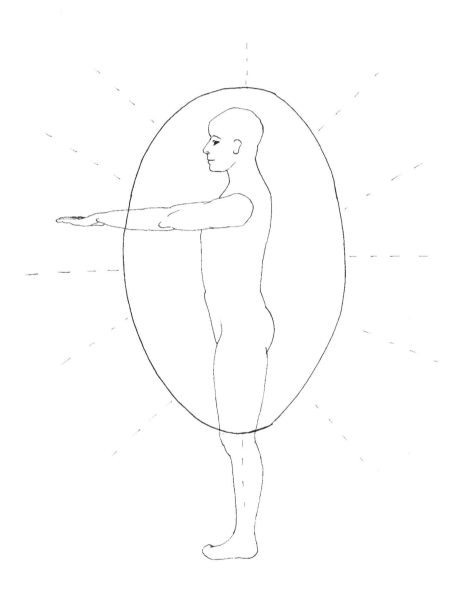

The chakra spheres have opened into a unified chakra field.
The mental body no longer blocks access to light from the higher
bodies. The lifeforce center has moved up to the heart.

The Seven Bodies of Man

*Masculine bodies are
electrical and feminine
bodies are magnetic in nature*

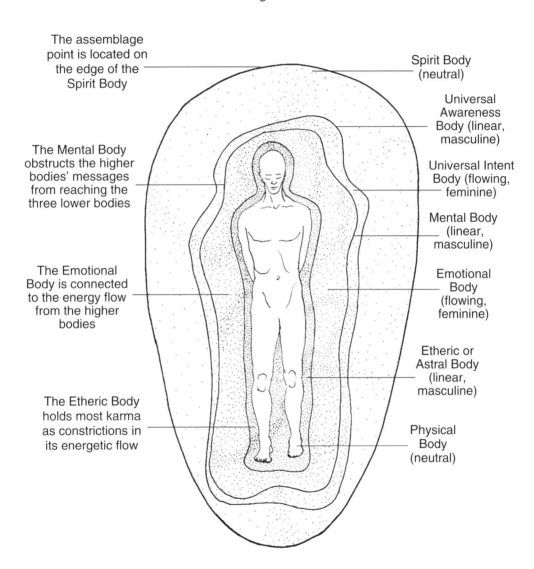

The assemblage point is located on the edge of the Spirit Body

Spirit Body (neutral)

Universal Awareness Body (linear, masculine)

The Mental Body obstructs the higher bodies' messages from reaching the three lower bodies

Universal Intent Body (flowing, feminine)

Mental Body (linear, masculine)

The Emotional Body is connected to the energy flow from the higher bodies

Emotional Body (flowing, feminine)

Etheric or Astral Body (linear, masculine)

The Etheric Body holds most karma as constrictions in its energetic flow

Physical Body (neutral)

The bodies are superimposed over each other and form the luminous egg (cocoon) of man. Death rolls against this egg and when this rolling force cracks the egg, its lifeforce spills out and the person dies.

however, it is specifically referring to the seven seals of the earth as they open for ascension.

The unified chakra field forms a low or almost non-existent electromagnetic field around the body, similar to being at a sacred site. Wherever we are becomes the most sacred place on the planet and our vibration heals those around us. This happens because the love we emit through our cells alters any distortions in the geometric fields around their bodies. They heal through grace. This is what we experience when we go to sacred sites. People go there because it also alters the way they look at the world. We have that same effect on people.

Beyond our physical body, we have lightbodies which are connected to the seven chakras. Before our seven chakras open, the mental body, which is connected to the ego, stands guard to block the information of the three higher spiritual bodies. The three spiritual bodies are the ones containing the blueprint for the full potential of our life. Clearing the debris from the chakras and forming a unified field gives us access to this blueprint. We then receive clear communication from all our bodies.

The five lightbodies that surround the physical body alternate between being masculine (linear) and feminine (flowing fields). They mimick the dimensions, with the outer-most one (the seventh body) and the physical body being neutral.

The Seven Bodies

1. **Physical Body:** The physical body is the anchoring point for your Higher Self to explore the mystery of your being within physicality. It is highly susceptible to programming transmitted through touch for several minutes after birth. It holds the memories of this and other lives.

2. **Etheric or Astral Body:** The majority of karma, which is a con-

striction in the universal flow of energy formed by incorrect perception, is held in the astral body (only a small portion is in the physical body). It consists of bluish lines of light. It produces the acupuncture points and the major and minor chakras by the energy lines crossing each other. Where they cross seven times, there is an acupuncture point. Where they cross 13 times, there is a minor chakra point. Where they cross 20 times, there is a major chakra point. This body is linear and is located an inch out from the physical body.

3. **Emotional Body:** It is the auric field. Past trauma is held in the first three bodies (the physical, astral, and emotional bodies), therefore, as we overcome our past and balance our subpersonalities[3], this body becomes clearer. This body is a flowing field that extends about 14 inches out from the physical body.

4. **Mental Body:** As we balance the three minds, including the left and right brains, the mental body ceases to block access to the higher bodies. This body is linear and is located about 14 inches out from the physical body.

5. **Universal Intent Body:** When able to access this body, we begin living in eternal time, which aligns us with the intent of the Infinite. This body is a flowing field that extends about 19 inches out from the physical body.

6. **Universal Awareness Body:** The information within this body contains the specifics regarding the blueprint for this lifetime. When access to this body is achieved, we start seeing from a cosmic perspective. We begin to see the innocence and value of each life as it mirrors to the Infinite either that which it is, or that which it is not. We see that there is no guilt so all judgment effortlessly dissolves. This body is linear and is located about 19 inches out from the physical body.

---

3 A description and the role of the subpersonalities are in "Connecting the Subpersonalities"

7. **Spirit Body:** It is trillions of little fibers of light radiating out in all directions from the lifeforce center[4] (located behind the bellybutton). Every living creature within the cosmos has a band of awareness among these light fibers within our spirit body. That is why we are literally the cosmos. This is the body shamans use to be able to shapeshift into animals or other forms; plus they use this body to access parallel realities. They move a point of illumination called the assemblage point. It is located an arm's length behind the heart, and a little bit to the right. This body is a linear field radiating out from the center to an arm's length from the physical body.

The assemblage point is on the outer rim of the seventh lightbody (spirit body) and is an illuminated spot that determines which reality we are in. If that point moves, this universe, which seems solid, disappears and another reality assembles. It is as though we have accessed different holographic experiences. A slight movement of the assemblage point puts us in an altered state, such as in meditation. With practice, we can go into a temporary meditative state, even if we are just going to the end of the garden to get the mail. It is a temporary disconnecting of the clamour of left-brain that allows pure information from higher realms to shed light on the situation and give us accurate information about the unknown.[5]

Our energy comes from bodies 5-7, consequently, if our innermost bodies have constrictions, we become tired easily because the flow of energy from the higher bodies is blocked. The emotional

---

4 The lifeforce center is a ball of white light about the size of a grapefruit.
5 For further information on developing these techniques, reference the "Path to Freedom" tape sets.

body is particularly important in allowing the flow of energy.

Beyond the Seven Bodies, we have five larger bodies, with the 12th body being the one as vast as the cosmos overlaying everything. As we move through the various stages of ascension, we fully activate all 12 lightbodies. At this point we function from 12 chakras instead of seven.

When all 12 bodies are accessed in this lifetime, we enlighten everything in all our lifetimes since they are all connected. Every past act and thought becomes perfected. This is an important factor because if we die we may leave ripples of discordance from sowing seeds that were less than loving. When we change the past, the present changes; and when the present changes, the past changes.

Grids Surrounding the Earth

A grid is a geometric array of light, and light is information. These grids surround the planet in geometric patterns. Each species has one and it is the "instinctual" information for that plant or animal. There are two grids around the earth that tell us how to be human. One is the old, third-dimensional fear based grid. The other is the Christ Consciousness grid, which is a fourth-dimensional, group-minded grid. It is the one that ascension is moving toward.

We are connected with all humans on the planet through the grids. The grids are connected to our hearts. That is how our thoughts, feelings and actions affect all of humanity.

One person's life lived gloriously can affect the grid around the planet and it becomes accessible to all beings. The mission of Jesus Christ included the formation of the Christ Consciousness grid. It was necessary to give humans an option other than functioning solely from the fear-based grid that contains a lot of negativity due to the age of dark materialism the earth has been in for approximately 13,000 years. For the past 2,000 years everyone has had the option to live from the higher consciousness grid. Furthermore, since Jesus formed the grid, all beings that have ascended have strengthened it.

That is why focusing within is the most important work we can do. When we understand that the decisions we make affect everyone, we realize it is important for us to be whole.

The Pause Between the Breaths

We are intimately connected with Mother Earth and she with us. If something happens to the earth, it changes humans, and vice versa, but it doesn't stop there. When the earth is healed it creates a ripple that continues throughout the universe.

Currently the lower dimensions of this universe are burdened with the weight of housing the dregs of the other universes. Our universe is the farthest from Source—it is as far as light can be taken into matter. The universe is like a tube toris, and during the out-breath of God, it folds out, and during the in-breath of God, it folds in. A tube toris is like a donut that rolls in upon itself, or we can imagine it as a metal coiled cylinder with its ends connected. The earth sits on the outer edge of this tube toris and it is stuck due to the massive amount of density it is holding.

The other universes cannot return to Source, even though they have fulfilled their purposes, because they are likewise stuck until the edge moves. We are the edge. Because of the apparent stalemate that exists here, we are the crucial point that will start the momentum of moving all of creation by folding over the edge of the tube toris, back toward the heart of God. That is why the earth is the hot-spot of all the universes. Consequently, the Lightworkers from every corner of every galaxy have sent their best to earth. In addition, those of the undeveloped light have sent their best too.

That, which appears to be "stuck" in the outward expansion of creation, seems so only from our limited perspective. It is in fact that moment during the blowing up of a balloon when it can expand no further, yet it continues to accept a bit more air. The friction against the wall of the balloon is the most intense, as is the discomfort at our level of existence. But this is part of the perfection of the plan. Think of it as the pause between the out-breath and the in-breath of God. The suffering we experience is held in the pause between our breaths. That is why re-birthing techniques are vey helpful: they release pent-up trauma through breathwork. This planet is vitally important because it has a contract to fulfill. The earth resolves the universe's unresolved pain, which is held in the pause between its breaths. She is rewarded for this great sacrifice by being the bride leading the bridal procession home. She will be the first to go from the red road away from the heart, onto the blue road back to the heart of God.

Task as a Human

Our task as a human begins this moment. Whatever we are doing, if it inspires the highest in us, it is an appropriate step. There is nothing wrong with studying any religious path or teaching, as long as it makes our heart sing. All paths lead up the mountain. However, there comes a point far up the mountain where all paths merge into one, and all that remains is the path of pure Spirit. That is the point where we leave the dogma, rituals and sacred objects behind. Anything we have used as a crutch will fall away. For we will see clearly that all true power lies within. We will never fulfill our destiny to become a clear channel for the light of God as long as we reach for anything outside ourselves.

Even the search for truth is an external pursuit, so eventually, that will cease because at the apex of the mountain, we realize that we are actually creating truth. Reality only appears fixed due to a peculiarity of our perception. When we change our perception, it changes reality. A master knows this and can alter his reality moment by moment.

There is No Destination

We are on a path that has no point of arrival because there is no destination. There is only the journey. Our journey through eternity offers us experiences so we may remember who we are—and that is God. To remember who we are, we must push beyond our comfort zone and break the barriers that lock us into the familiar, leaving us with a sense of false security. If we remain in our comfort zone, we become stagnant.

The only thing worth striving for is clarity. We don't search for meaning because we understand that the majority of the universe is unknowable. Clarity pertains to our next step only as we seek to gather insights from our experiences.

We gain the pearls of wisdom from our uncomfortable human experiences, until we are able to pull free from the fear that causes the discomfort. We continue this inner cleansing until we have removed layer after layer of fear. In doing this, we push our perception until it moves beyond mortal boundaries. This desire to push the perimeter of the known is what is called living a path with heart or living on the crest of the wave.

When there is no destination, it follows that there is also no preferable point along the journey. Therefore, one in separation consciousness is as important in the big picture as one who has realized he is all things. Both are equally perfect.

Humility is crucial as we walk the spiritual path. If we imagine the path as an unending ladder that spirals upward, any belief system only takes us up one rung. If we choose to remain in the role of master on a particular rung, then we become stuck. When we have mastered one rung, that is the signal for the universe to bump us up to the next rung, where we are a student again.

Being vs Doing

One of the most difficult concepts to grasp is that it doesn't matter what we do. People constantly ask, "What is my work on earth?" You can be sweeping the streets or be an executive in a corporation or heal the sick and it all has the same value.

Many people fall into the trap of thinking their work is important. They even think work is their life. Many wonderful Lightworkers run around doing what they perceive as their life's mission—feeling that the world won't be the same if they don't complete that mission.

Anything associated with doing activities and perpetuating identity labels is the work of the surface mind. They are labels such as: I am a teacher; I am an artist; I am a healer; or I help people. There is no important work; there are only a series of moments to behave impeccably. If we obsess about doing, our connection with Spirit is severed because Spirit is accessed through our state of being.

As long as you are focused on work that is outside yourself, you will never be in your power because all true power lies within. The greatest changes to this planet can only occur through your inner being functioning from your heart center. It isn't what you do that counts, it is who you are. That is your greatest contribution to mankind because it is your attitude that registers in the grid of humanity.

Even the words "your greatest contribution to mankind" are meaningless when we fully understand the concept of the spiderweb. If you are sitting in the middle of your spiderweb and you have aligned yourself over the universal spiderweb, in other words, you have aligned yourself with universal intent, every single thought ripples throughout the universe. Thus, be careful not to get tangled in one thread by thinking your actions are important. By being who you are and vibrating at that frequency, you can affect all of creation. You will feel a sense of freedom when you release the draining experiences of trying to save the world and others.

Mankind has one responsibility and that is to be. However, the star-seeded beings have agreed to take on one additional responsibility, and that is to show others how to be, since many have forgotten. That is why there is nothing more important than reflecting the wisdom of our life into the informational grid of humanity by returning to who we are, which is love. As we live daily at this level of awareness, all humans who tap into the grid will be uplifted.

We have to make the choice to walk in the light or not, because it takes determination to release our beliefs that have become our prison bars. It takes courage and dedication to choose the path of a wayshower, for it is a lonely path. The social tribe rejects us and the majority of our friends may fall by the wayside.

Masks vs Identities

While in our state of expanded awareness, it is okay to wear different masks but not to take them seriously. We understand that a mask is merely that, but an identity is a mask we believe. For example, a woman wears a mask of a court judge. The mask is fine as long as she knows it isn't who she is. It is appropriate for her to wear that mask as long as needed, and then merely release it, with no emotion or judgment attached.

A Master's Life is Disciplined

As the path of ascension unfolds, it becomes clear that we have earned the right to be powerful. Power is earned by achieving clarity and this occurs through living a disciplined life. However, this discipline is never imposed from the outside. It is the constant vigilance to eradicate the things that withhold your personal power from you.

One example would be people's thoughts. They are scattered, darting here and there, into the future, the past, opposing spoken words, judging or analyzing.

'How to' hint: See yourself as having reins on your surface mind, and pull back on them when your thoughts start running wild. No matter how many times a day you have to jerk on those reins and tell your mind to focus. Some days it may be almost non-stop! But you are training the mind.

Rampant thoughts prevent us from accessing our power. Through monitoring our thoughts, we can control our brain waves and enter that place of deep peace and inner stillness. With practice, we reach the point of constantly living in a meditative state and we no longer have a need to know; or a need to act; or a need to form an opinion; or have an expectation. We know there is a time to make a decision and a time not to—a time to act and a time not to. This is living innocently as a master in the present moment.

Living in the Moment

The realization that our purpose is "to be" and that Spirit will reveal to us when we need to act, is liberating. It frees us from striving for a specific outcome. We can relax with the confidence that we will be guided to act when appropriate and that we can truly focus on the moment, the place of all power.

The present moment is the position in the center of the figure eight of time where the loop of the past and the loop of the future meet. The Mayans called it the zuvuya. In relation to the physical body, the two loops meet in the lifeforce center, which for most people is located behind the bellybutton. Since time travels in loops, where we have been we will be again, and where we are going, we have already been. The loops are spiraling upward so each time we travel the loop, it is a little higher in awareness.

The lifeforce center is the power point within the physical body. During the ascension process it will rise to the heart center.

When we resist the moment, a thought forms. Thoughts place us either in the future or the past, which throws us off-balance and into a weakened state. We cannot become a master as long as we resist life. To concern ourselves about yesterday, tomorrow or the next three steps on our path is a waste of energy. If we feel anxious or pressured, we are missing the fact that everything is perfect and we have forgotten that we all have what we need to fulfill our life's blueprint.

Living in the moment initially brings with it some disconcerting side effects. The biggest one is loss of memory. We may have difficulty remembering yesterday. Even recalling what happened hours ago could be taxing. I may say, "Last week I went to the beach," and my son will correct me, "but Mother, that was yesterday!" It may as well have been last week, for I have experienced a thousand present moments since yesterday.

Another factor contributing to the loss of memory is the fact that linear time is collapsing because it is connected with the earth's electromagnetic fields, and those fields are deteriorating.

Power is a Gift

Power is illusive in nature and isn't something we seek directly. It is the result of a balanced life: no longer being controlled by the past; free of personal identities or world views; having harmony among all the subpersonalities and minds; being free of fear; having no personal agenda or attachment to outcome. The universe doesn't entrust limitless power to those who haven't mastered themselves.

It is ironic that to reclaim our power, we have to no longer desire it. Personal desire is an emotional attachment to outcome. Once we are free of personal desires we can become a clear instrument for the divine will of Spirit. At that point, we only need to state our intention to allow power to flow through us. This principle applies across the board, for we won't be an effective teacher until we no longer desire to speak; we won't be an effective healer until we realize there is nothing or nobody to heal.

We cannot skip the steps on how to heal ourselves if we wish to become a teacher, healer or a master of power. We may have been granted a few natural abilities, but we become stuck at that level unless we become whole.

Another prerequisite to receiving limitless power is that we have reverence for all lifeforms. Any kingdom that could be affected by the abuse of power, has to be honored before that power can be granted. That means we need to honor the animal, plant, and mineral kingdoms, plus all lifeforms from other dimensions.

There are various techniques to force the acquisition of power. Many shamans use rituals, mind-altering drugs, or even a technique to cut the third-eye open, to force their way in. Sometimes a teacher pushes a student into expanded abilities. This may place the student in a precarious situation, for if he is still holding on to any fear, it will manifest. The student shouldn't be in that position until he has become whole and has elevated his perspective.

Therefore, if we find ourselves drop-shipped to the top of the mountain, know that we have to come back down and learn our lessons. These glimpses of power are intoxicating and often we don't wish to return and deal with our personal issues. But there are no shortcuts to God realization. That is why we must first gain love and wisdom, before we reach the place of power. Once you have earned the right to have power, then you need never be afraid. For the light of God within you is thousands of times more potent than anything the undeveloped light may send your way.

Power Seekers vs Perception Seekers

Power is the result of altered perception. The key word is "result," because if we seek power directly, we are on a dead-end street. Let us look at the differences between those who are seeking power and those who are seeking clarity of perception.

Power Seekers
• Seek power directly

- Focus on power
- Purpose of power is to manipulate energy to be able to see into the future and the past. It is power over the environment and power beyond another's abilities.
- Enhance self-image, which is strengthened by titles and labels
- View perception as a result of the use of power
- Obsess about the unseen realms and the unknown
- Get power from outside sources, such as allies
- Measure themselves by what they are doing

Perception Seekers

- Seek clarity
- Focus on perception
- Purpose of power is to break free from mortal boundaries and gain God realization.
- Eliminate self-importance and shun labels which trap awareness
- View power as a result of perception
- Seek more refined goals until the unknowable is reached.
- Get power from living in the awareness of the inter-connectedness of all life. They access the attributes an ally could provide by going within, since all life is within. They draw upon these sources as if they are themselves.
- Measure themselves by how they are being

When we obtain personal power, it becomes a challenge because we are able to perform miracles. The temptation is to impress others, and if we succumb to this, we are choosing the way of the power seekers. This is the point where a Lightworker has to choose to walk either the humble and unobtrusive road that leads to complete freedom, or the dead-end road of showmanship. Most choose the flashy road, but it is of little value except to enhance the ego of the performer.

A miracle shouldn't be planned. It occurs naturally when we are pushing the boundaries of mortality. Miracles shouldn't be performed to persuade, demonstrate, or to gain approval or raise the status of the teacher. Power seekers often use showy miracles to encourage faith in the followers. The increased faith is focused on the power seeker and it creates a momentum to further feed his abilities, hence, providing him with additional power.

Power seekers can get trapped in identity labels such as a shaman, sorcerer, or medicine man. If they become arrogant and fall into the trap of "thinking they know," they can get stuck in the unknown and won't be able to access the unknowable. This is a limiting position because the known comprises 1/12th of the universe and the unknown comprises 11/12ths of the universe. Both of these are within creation. On the other hand, the unknowable is outside of creation—it is that which is dreaming creation into existence. A perception seeker's goal is to access the unknowable. That is why they focus on clarity of perception and strive to shed limiting labels and beliefs. They understand there is no point of arrival. This type of fluidity allows the perception seeker the freedom to be all things.

The perception seekers practice a shamanism that predates the Fall of Consciousness, that according to ancient oral traditions happened 9,564 years before the crucifixion of Jesus Christ.

The Unknown

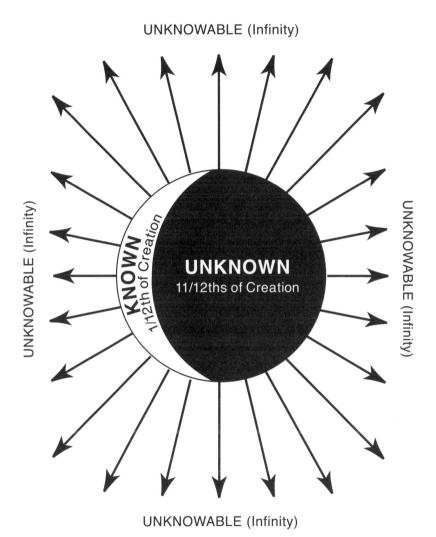

Changing Your Perspective

Welcome Change

If we don't take responsibility for our actions, we cannot move forward. The first guideline to achieve this is to realize the environment is a mirror of what is going on inside us. When we change our perception, our environment changes. The secret is to welcome change, and change occurs through life's challenges.

It is amazing how fervently people avoid challenges. Yet it is the only place where growth can occur. If we allow ourselves to continue habitual patterns, we become stagnant. Many of the indigenous people hunted only the deer that repeated the same behaviors day-after-day. The hunters knew these deer were stuck in a rut and therefore had less lifeforce energy. They were easier to hunt and had less energy to pass on to the next generation. Doing the same activities every day constricts energy, so be wary of habits and strive to break them.

It is crucial to understand that the greatest perspective may be gained by the challenge that shows us who we are not, so we can more fully understand who we are. The challenges we embrace don't have to be painful. As we become more adept at seeing behind appearances[6], we can learn the lessons effortlessly.

There are three ways to learn. The first way is to heed the gentle prodding of Spirit. This may appear as an intuitive instruction, an inner voice, or visual signs while we are awake or during the dreamstate. The second way is to wait for the hard knocks, when it seems as though Spirit is hitting us over the head with a 2X4. That

6 In ancient shamanic traditions, this is called sobriety.

is Spirit's way of asking, "Do you want to wake up from this nightmare?" The third way is by grace. Grace allows an instantaneous waking up. When grace occurs, those things that are dysfunctional in our lives stand out like sore thumbs, begging to be brought into harmony. Living in grace allows us to hear the whispers of Spirit and make decisions based on the highest reflection of who we are.

If we learn to embrace the challenges that bring change to our doorstep, our spiritual journey will be greatly accelerated. Remember, a challenge is merely a piece of the mystery of being that we have, as yet, not solved. The bravest prayer I know is to ask God to show you your greatest fear. If you do, it will happen. If we embrace each step as it unfolds, we experience tremendous growth. For within our challenges lie our deepest insights, and insight brings power. Therefore, our challenges are power sources.

Changing Truths

While learning to embrace change, it is important not to get stuck on one set of truths. Today's truth isn't tomorrow's truth, therefore, hold on lightly to your beliefs. Truths change as our perception changes because reality is merely an interpretation. That is why when you ask me what I believe, I say I believe in nothing. I may know many things, but that may change tomorrow.

Physics has taught us to discount the magic behind life to such an extreme extent that we believe the only things that are real are those that can be proven with our limited tools or experienced through the senses. This isn't accurate. Reality only appears fixed due to a peculiarity of our perception.

Linear time is an example of a peculiarity of perception. The more dense the planet, the longer the gap between cause and effect. We created this dense planet to give ourselves time to make mistakes and experience the unknown parts of ourselves.

The third-dimensional reality appearing solid is another peculiarity. What we see is dependent on where the assemblage point is located. Humans have their assemblage points stuck at approximately the same position, that is why we see more or less the same reality. If any of us move our assemblage point far enough, this reality disappears.

These types of peculiarities cause the world to appear as an unalterable maze that we have to navigate through without a guidebook. Hence, we spend our lives seeking truth. But the universe responds to our thoughts and feelings. Indeed, a master creates truth. Therefore, the goal isn't to seek truth, but to create it consciously.

Later today a host of angels may bring an answer to a question that we have asked for years. That single piece of information may cause us to be bumped up to the next rung of our spiritual ladder, and our truth may be altered when seen from that heightened perspective. Inner stillness is necessary so that when our answer arrives, we are able to hear it. Also, remain humble enough not to judge the information by the person who delivers it. A deluded brother might bring the answer, and even though on the surface it may appear to contradict the angels, we need to recognize it as our new truth. There is a wise saying, "Even a clock that is broken is correct twice a day."

No Hierarchy of Importance

We are all the One expressing as the many. We all exist in many dimensions simultaneously so importance doesn't apply. There is no hierarchy in terms of importance. That means the little rose fairy in the garden has the same importance as Archangel Michael. Archangel Michael's task might be viewed as a greater, more complex assignment with a broader range of ramifications, but their significance is the same.

Humility is recognizing that within the mystery of God's being, all are equal. Every being contributes a unique equation that enhances God's understanding of the mystery of His being. If one number is removed from the equation then it no longer works.

One may say, "Look, we aren't created equal. There are people out there who are killing each other and people who don't have talents or intelligence." That is an illusion based on not being able to see how valuable their role is in the big picture. What is important to grasp is that everyone's inner-essence and contribution is of equal value.

So what is the difference between star beings and someone else? When the I AM started to create itself into forms, the majority of the souls came to earth walking down a staircase, coming down many steps to get to this density. That is the case with John Doe, the average man on the street. John Doe is the manifestation of God, with the ability to return to Source, and again become God, but he may not choose to develop that ability in this life.

John Doe who descended via the long staircase is removed from remembering his oneness with Source by up to trillions of years. The Lightworkers and the majority of star beings came from Source in only a few steps, but slowly enough to begin to adjust to the lower vibrations. Therefore, it is easier for them to remember their Godhood because their sense of separation is less.

When star beings come to earth and ascend as an individual, they hook into large soul-groups, meaning they become archetypal. What they do ripples throughout the entire group. When they overcome life's challenges and remember who they are, it makes it easier for the group to do likewise. These star beings will carry a larger number of beings along during the mass ascension. When we raise one group of beings up, the others must rise too because we are like mountain climbers, attached by a rope.

A handful of star-seeded beings descended like a meteorite. We came from the highest heavens where we lived in light and purity of thought and plunged into the densest density. That means one minute we were the highest and the next minute we were the lowest, which is a painful experience. That rapid plunge is referred to in the angelic kingdom as the greatest fear in the universe.

CHAPTER THREE

REVEALING THE PERFECTION

Our Duty is to be Whole

It is our sacred duty to be healthy and whole, otherwise we send a discordant ripple throughout the consciousness of mankind via the grids. Sickness is indicative of something being out of balance.

Healing isn't merely removing a physical symptom. We need to look at why it is out of balance because our aches and pains are Spirit's way of signaling us to deal with the root of the problem. Spirit says through the language of pain, "This aspect needs to be brought back into harmony."

The body desires all its parts to be functioning in perfect harmony, that is why it alerts us when something needs to be brought into alignment. Be aware that this includes our emotions, thoughts and actions. If anything is out of balance, it eventually manifests in the physical body.

If we develop a sickness or disease or injure ourselves, keep in mind that we created it. Spirit attempts to get our attention in subtle ways at first. If we repeatedly choose to ignore the gentle prodding, it gets our attention through aches and pains to the physical body.

When we embrace the root problem and correct it, the pain goes away. Wholeness is what remains when we heal ourselves on every level: mentally, emotionally and physically. However, becoming balanced on all these levels is no easy task, for during this incarnation we are integrating all our lifetimes and solving all the problems incurred during each. As a result, we need to be patient with ourselves and realize that we walk the spiral of healing over and over, until not one cobweb from one lifetime remains.

Healing Others

Throughout history there have been times when using energetic healing was outlawed. Women were labeled as witches and millions were burned at the stake or ostracized. At a cellular level, our body has memory of this, therefore, it takes courage to stand up and claim our ability to heal.

Assisting others to heal is a great service but we need to keep in mind that ultimately, everyone heals himself. So the highest service is to show others how to make themselves whole, then we have co-created another healer. It is the principle of helping others to help themselves: "If someone is starving, don't give him corn. Teach him how to grow it."

If we simply healed without educating the person about why the disease has manifested, the same problem will appear again in a few weeks, months or in a couple of years. It may return as a reoccurrence of the original physical problem or it may manifest somewhere else.

If we heal without guidance as to cause, we aren't honoring the fact that he masterfully manifested that condition for potential personal growth. His spirit is saying, "Please get your life into balance and fully live who you are—a being as vast as the cosmos." If we deprive him of the opportunity, it is an injustice. We would be seeing him as a helpless person who needs to be rescued. However, if the client chooses to embrace the lesson, his perception alters and increased power, peace and good health will be his reward.

You are Immune to Everything

Ultimately, when we live at our highest level, we are completely immune to everything. When we are centered and have stable personal boundaries, we don't get sick. But if we slip into limiting thought patterns, we are a likely candidate for an injury, infection or illness.

One of the seeming drawbacks of being a Lightworker is that the more highly evolved we become, the less tolerant our vibration is of any negative energy. That means the slightest limiting thought immediately manifests in the physical. This isn't something to fear, it is something to be aware of.

Nobody is a Victim

It is impossible for us to be victims. Spirit sends nothing but lessons or gifts, and from a higher perspective, they are both the same. If God sends nothing but good, how can we be victims?

Once we fully grasp that we are all things—not just the physical body—then we know that everyone and all things are within us. Nobody can do something to us if they dwell within us. Even God's lessons and gifts are what we called forth to unfold the mystery of our unknown pieces.

There simply cannot be anything in this universe that doesn't promote the intention of the Infinite to explore the mystery of its being. Even the undeveloped light has the most profound effect in helping us grow by offering us opportunities to change our perspective. Remember, without friction, we cannot walk; without resistance, there is no evolution. There can be no evil, only delusion.

One of the biggest fallacies on earth is that another person can do anything to us; that another person is responsible for what happens to us. This isn't possible because we create every circumstance in our life. It was placed there so we can see ourselves reflected back and know what areas still need to be brought into the light. We cannot take anything personally, even if something is said that appears to be an assault on our character. If we react to words, even with a minute twinge, then there is something that still needs to be dealt with.

When people begin to accept that they create their own reality, they wonder how horrific things can happen to an innocent child. We cannot say that a little girl who was molested, consciously brought it about. It occurred as a result of the negative group consciousness. However, it is important to understand that on a soul level, she did volunteer to experience it. That is the sacred duty the girl agreed to undergo prior to her incarnation. When she chooses such an experience and overcomes it, she is providing a service because it raises the consciousness of mankind, or her agreement may have been with an individual, to act as a mirror for him to learn a lesson.

We Create Our Reality

Our most prominent thought coupled with feeling is really a prayer and it is that which creates our reality. Thoughts flow into the reservoir of the heart and act upon the substance of things hoped for. It is a living, delicate substance that fills the entire universe and responds to our thoughts and feelings. Thoughts come alive when they are coupled with feeling and it sets in motion that which results in physical manifestation.

One of the powers of creation is that a mindset reproduces itself. If we spend all day fearful of being audited by the IRS and then at night we ask, "Oh God, please help," what is more prevalent, that which we thought all day or the few pleading words for help?

It is important that we start taking absolute responsibility for our lives and the condition of the world. We also created the seemingly imperfect conditions on our planet through our limited thoughts. When millions of people are thinking negative thoughts, it registers on the grid and they become easier to manifest.

Guarding our thoughts has become more imperative than ever. Especially since the time lapse between what we think and its physical manifestation is becoming shorter each year as we approach 2013. This is the result of the deterioration of the electromagnetic fields surrounding the earth.

When we realize we create our destiny, we know we are in control of our abundance. God wishes us to have abundance, wealth and beauty. However, He created us with the ability to create it for ourselves. We must learn to trust in ourselves and know that we are the Source that breathed life into ourselves—the I AM THAT I AM. Then we can lie back in the arms of Spirit and simply be, having faith that we will be taken care of.

What We Resist Persists

Attention feeds energy, so we empower that which we focus on and we attract that which we fear. These are some of the hidden laws of the universe.

Some are laboring diligently to change the world in an attempt to correct what they think is wrong. The error in that reasoning is: we strengthen that which we oppose. The more we focus on a problem, the more we empower it. For example, when the media sensationalizes a situation, it promotes more of the same. Even though it is presented as opposition, they are still strengthening it because they are giving it energy. The same is true if we continually focus on a disease—we magnify it. In addition, the negative thoughts weaken our auric field and we become susceptible to other harmful things. If we don't feed something, however, it grows weaker and weaker.

When we attempt to right a wrong, it divides because we have placed a judgment on it as not being in alignment with the divine will of Spirit. This is separative thinking. However, if we acknowledge the wholeness of a circumstance or person, it will uplift and heal. This is inclusive thinking.

We cannot return to Source as long as we exclude anything. This doesn't mean we condone unworthy acts, but recognize instead, the innocence of all roles being acted out for our benefit. This helps us see that only light exists and we can drop the belief that there are places where God is not. It is in recognizing the dark as part of ourselves that we can embrace it within our hearts, and as we find ourselves returning to the oneness of the heart of God, we take those that represent the dark with us.

In the past I had staff members not wanting to deal with victims of ritual abuse and demon possessions. They claimed, "That is the dark and we only want to work with the light." I replied, "But we are all things, so we are also those things."

Another example is a friend in London who works against child slavery. Child slave labor is prevalent in the Orient, India, and South America. Children are forced to labor long days and often don't receive any money, only food and shabby shelter as payment. Many of the girls end up as sex slaves or working in the tapestry mills where they cannot earn enough money to support themselves. They are then stuck for life at the mercy of their employers.

Many parents are tricked. The slave-trader comes to a village and says, "Give your children to me so I can educate them. Look at this photo of these healthy, happy kids dressed in uniforms, studying their books." So the parents are persuaded to allow their children to go with these people because they think they are going to school. The way to combat this is to not combat it. A better approach is to shed light onto the situation by making people aware. Use information to inform parents of what is really happening to their children. Expose the conditions of the children to the public through the mass media. As readers or viewers become aware, it creates a wave of compassion and that wave of energy will start to alter the circumstances.

By all means let us do whatever Spirit places before us, but let us strive to see with the eyes of God and act without judging or having an attachment to the outcome. Let us remember that all is in divine order.

Language of Pain

At a spiritual level, all illness, pain, disease, and injuries are the language of Spirit telling us what aspect of our lives needs to be brought into harmony with who we are. Therefore, it is wise to examine what is behind the symptom and ask for the lesson, then embrace it and release it. When we release core issues, the illness, pain or disease goes away.

If there is no need for the language of pain to get our attention, we won't become sick. Nobody causes another person to get sick. A sickness that is labeled contagious certainly has the potential to spread, but it cannot invade the body if we are balanced and have healthy boundaries. The only time a germ or virus slips in, is if we have forsaken ourselves by doing things such as suppressing the subpersonalities or engaging in self-deprecating thoughts or beliefs. We become immune to disease when we balance the emotional body and we are home for ourselves by reconnecting the subpersonalities and allowing them freedom of expression.

Accidents don't occur to those who walk in balance. If we have no cause for an accident to manifest, we will walk in grace, even if we are in the center of an earthquake or hurricane. The language of pain includes injuries from accidents, because in truth, there is no such thing as an accident. We masterfully manifested the incident.

If pain is the language of Spirit, what is the language of the soul? It is our feelings. When we have done something that feels wonderful, we have just lived our highest truth. If we follow our feelings, we automatically walk our highest truth.

'**Note**'–Spirit as used in this context, pertains to our Highest Self as a being as vast as the cosmos. It is when we aren't remembering this true identity that dis-ease occurs. Soul, on the other hand, relates to our Higher Self, our fourth-dimensional aspect that has designed our assignments for this life. It communicates the assignments to our higher bodies, which in turn communicates it to our emotional body (assuming the mental body lets these messages through). Then it is felt in the heart.

We must be careful when it comes to feelings, though, because fears can masquerade as feelings. Feelings are also frequently confused with emotions. I would like to clarify this so when we are analyzing the language of pain, we know the difference.

Feelings vs Emotions

Feeling is a way to access information that isn't accessible to reason. It bypasses the mind. Therefore, feeling is a non-cognitive way of getting information, which registers as an intuitive knowing. Feeling is the right-brain accessing the unknown. It deals with things beyond the five senses and logic.

Emotion has as its foundation, desire. There are only four true emotions and all other emotions are combinations of these:

Four True Emotions
1. Joy is the desire to live.
2. Fear is the desire to retreat.
3. Anger is the desire to attack.
4. Sadness is the desire to change.

Before feelings are beneficial for accessing the unknown, they must be free of emotion. The key to accomplishing this is learning to feel emotion without attachment to the outcome. If we see starving children or ghastly war crimes on the TV, just observe without being influenced. Remember that there is no need for us to judge because those people aren't their experiences.

Allow yourself to experience emotions, but only on the surface, keeping in mind that it is just a storm in a teacup since the whole bottom of the ocean is completely peaceful. Expressing passionately is essential to keeping the meridians open and creating a low electromagnetic density around the body that can be equated to a sacred space. It also keeps the emotional body clear. Therefore, express your emotions fully, but recognize them for what they are—a tool to push back density.

It is okay to have strong emotions as long as you release them in a constructive way that isn't threatening to yourself or others. I actually enjoy the surface storms because I am not attached to anger or malice or hatred or recrimination. I feel safe within my emotions.

A step beyond that is to simply experience them. For example, if a challenge causes me pain, this is how I hurt: I don't resist. I don't analyze. I don't try to change it. I just experience the emotion. Consequently, I am not afraid of hurting because it will pass right through me and won't become stuck. With this attitude one isn't afraid to make oneself vulnerable with a partner or deeply loving one's children. One isn't afraid of being rejected or hurt, because feeling hurt is the same as feeling the joy—one isn't bad and the other good.

'How to' hint: When experiencing a painful situation, don't analyze it while you are feeling the initial emotion. That clouds judgment. Just experience the emotion. Afterwards, when you are calm and can access the feeling without it being colored by emotion, then use your left-brain to see behind the appearances so you can embrace the lesson. (If we are tangled up in emotions, we may miss the core lesson and then we have to create a similar circumstance later.)

To change our emotions, we need to alter our perception. It works in reverse too, because altering emotion causes altered perception. The two work hand-in-hand.

It is necessary for the sake of clarity to explain the meaning of the word love, as used here: Divine love is a state of being that remains when all fear is removed. At a higher level, love isn't an emotion. It isn't a feeling, nor a desire. It is a vibration in the cells that resonates with the intent of the universe. And the intent of the universe is to include all of creation within itself. Divine love is unconditional.

We don't need to worry about how to generate it because we already are love. Simply remove all fear by seeing behind the appearances and the filter obstructing love will be removed.

Sentimental love is a joyous emotion that results from believing that another completes us. We may choose a partner who brings in what we don't have, or haven't developed yet, or have given away. Consequently, in his or her presence we experience wholeness. It is a false sense of wholeness, but it can elicit joy. That explains why some people feel they have no identity away from the union as a couple. The same feeling of joy that results from sentimental love, can be developed within ourselves by balancing our emotional aspects.

Compassion is a response of empathy to another's emotions and the subsequent interpretation of it. Unlike divine love, the compassionate response to another changes as perception alters, taking on different forms along the rungs of enlightenment.

Interpreting the Language of Pain

The following list of body parts and symptoms will assist us in recognizing the areas of our lives that are out of balance.

General areas and systems of the body:

Breath indicates our ability to express ourselves in life. If we don't express ourselves, it is as though someone has placed a boulder on our chest and we cannot fully breathe. Frequently, people place the boulder on themselves.

The breath is expressing our lifeforce, so **asthma** patients have lifeforce problems. Often they were stifled from expressing as children. Babies and toddlers know the big picture of who they are, so they may experience tremendous frustration over being trapped in a physical body, unable to express the glory of their true identity. It is helpful to assist children to find safe avenues to explore their gifts and talents. When the lifeforce becomes suppressed, the exhaling process becomes difficult, as is the case with asthma.

> **'How to' hint:** Asthma patients may find it helpful to blow-up balloons as a means to strengthen the muscles involved in exhaling. One way to be consistent is to blow-up approximately eight balloons each time you use the toilet.

The **fluids** of our body have to do with emotions. **Blood**, in particular, is the equivalent of love. The ability to love is very important. If we deliberately withhold love we find constriction in our arteries. **Hardened arteries** mean hardened emotions.

The **heart** has to do with giving love. The energy we give is supposed to enter our body through the crown chakra, from the limitless supply of the universe, and flow out through our heart. If we close our heart because of fear or from not being fully present in our body, then we begin to give energy from our lifeforce center. This depletes us.

In order to insulate ourselves from this drain of energy, a layer of fat could build up around the solar plexus (stomach area). Lightworkers frequently have this layer of fat as an attempt to protect their energy source. People who suffered childhood abuse may use **fat** to insulate themselves from other people.

It is important to live fully in the body. Many people have suffered childhood sexual abuse and learned to leave the body when things got unpleasant. If we don't stay in the body and feel, then the heart center remains closed and we cannot fulfill our highest calling on this planet.

Soft tissues and ligaments reflect attitudes. Is our attitude positive? Do we frequently complain? The **joints** have to do with how flexible we are. The soft tissues control the joints, so they are affected too. For example, in the past, prior to a seminar I would receive the topic but no specific information on the forthcoming lecture. As a result, my knee joints hurt because I wasn't flexible enough to trust that I would receive the information at the appropriate time.

The **skin** reflects how we interface with the world. When the skin is irritated, it is because we perceive the world as abrasive or hostile. If a **boil** develops, that means a specific area of our life is like a sore.

Bones indicate what we inherited from our parents and ancestors, or what we received from genetic memory and early social conditioning.

If an ailment occurs on the **front** of the body, that means we are aware of the issue but we haven't dealt with it yet. If the ailment is on the **back** of the body, we are trying to put it behind us, or we aren't aware of it yet. If it is on the **left** side of the body, it has to do with our feminine aspects, or with female relationships in our life. Problems on the **right** side of the body reflect the masculine part of ourselves, or our masculine relationships.

A **virus** is the result of being invaded—our boundaries have broken down. The first and foremost sacred space for us is our body and we honor ourselves by establishing healthy boundaries and maintaining it.

Viruses, bacteria and fungus invade when our subpersonalities aren't healthy, happy, whole and functioning. Fungus tends to come when we have abandoned ourselves, bacteria invades when deliberate hostile influences are entering our boundaries and viruses are the result of others being allowed to use and abuse us.

Specific body parts:

The **head** signals thoughts and ideals—the way we think life ought to be. The **face** has to do with what we are presenting to the world. If our presentation is different from what is actually happening inside, our two "faces" are in conflict. As a result, **acne** may develop.

If we have negative thoughts, resentment, and feelings of being inadequate, mucous will develop in the **sinuses**. Phlegm, the fluid in the **throat**, is also an indication of negative emotions. **Headaches** often constitute repression of memories. They can also signify a conflict between the left and right brains.

For example, our right-brain knows that we are all-powerful beings—that every one of us is a consciousness superimposed over All That Is. If the left-brain opposes it, we develop a head-ache. (Learning about sacred geometry[7] eases this struggle because the left-brain will be reminded of what the right-brain already knows.)

Ear problems can mean there are things in our environment that we don't wish to hear: abusive language from a spouse; nagging from a mother; or disrespect from a child. When we protect our boundaries, yet realize that we cannot control the behavior of others, this heals. It is also helpful to see the abuse as their reflection, not ours, so that we don't take it personally.

The **thyroid** is where we suppress anger at not being heard. If there are pieces of our reality that don't fit, and we try to ignore

7 For more information on sacred geometry, reference "Journey into the Heart of God" III tape set.

them, it effects the thyroid.

Teeth and their roots are connected to bones, therefore, they indicate conflicts with parental figures or societal attitudes. Teeth have to do with how palatable parental teachings were. If we cannot accept a life situation, our teeth may become hyper-sensitive. Teeth also pertain to the need for aggression.

Problems with **gums** indicate something we cannot swallow in life. It is stuck and bothering us, so it becomes an abscess in the mouth.

The **neck** is where thoughts and ideals meet—reflecting the way life is for us. Lightworkers often have neck problems because the way they would like life to be and the way life appears, is at variance. That conflict meets in the neck.

A lot of people have **atlas** problems, meaning the head isn't on straight. This indicates a dramatic conflict between ideal and reality and an inability to embrace the folly of mankind. If we can start to see the perfection underlying all things, by looking at the larger picture, this conflict goes away.

The **shoulders, arms and hands** reflect that which is done to us or that which we are doing to another. The **hands** indicate the present moment. **Arms** mean it may be less obvious or more under the surface. **Shoulders** indicate that we have been trying to push it into the past.

If our feelings were hurt today, it manifests in the **fingers**. If we are still hurting over something that happened last week, it will possibly manifest in the **arm**, up toward the elbow. If there are issues from our childhood or from past relationships that we suppress, we find that in the **shoulders** or **back**.

Specific areas of the hands indicate different things. The **top joint** or section of the fingers has to do with ideals and the mental. The **middle joint** has to do with emotional issues. The **lower joint** has to do with the physical body. For example, when someone is hostile towards our spiritual beliefs and makes fun of a sacred object or a spiritual book we hold dear, we may develop a problem with the top joint of the finger. If someone makes fun of our intellect or our ability to solve problems, it also manifests in the top joint. One young woman who had developed a huge tumor in the brain came to me. Her husband's favorite nickname for her was "brain dead." That was an insult to the mental and she continually injured the top joints of her fingers.

The area **below the shoulders down to the hips** has to do with our desires and passion and our self-expression of the things we love to do. **Liver** problems indicate anger. **Kidney** problems indicate fear. **Sacrum** problems indicate that we feel unsupported.

The **hip** area is where we balance between how we desire to live and how we are actually living. For example, a man wants to be an artist but his parents forced him to become a lawyer. Therefore, he develops problems in the hips.

The **pubis** bone can lock in the front because there is cartilage that should move, and if it doesn't, it throws the back out of alignment. It locks when our sexuality is being drained. For example, when a young boy is expected to be the man in the family, he may start to shield his masculinity because he feels his energy being drained. If a woman is abused sexually, the pubis will lock.

Sexual organs relate to our ability to be active in reproduction.

Legs reflect how we are moving forward through life. The man who becomes a lawyer instead of an artist may also be prone to hurting his legs. Since his artistic talent is part of his feminine side, and the masculine is crowding it out, it will likely manifest in his left leg.

Knees reflect our flexibility towards what is happening to us. For example, a woman may have a sore right knee when she is being inflexible with her husband.

Problems with the **feet** indicate how we are moving through life in the present moment. For example, a man has many wonderful ideas at his job but his boss won't give him the freedom to follow those ideas, so his masculine side becomes stuck. He may have a car accident and jam the bones of his masculine foot, because his life is jammed from moving forward at this time.

Your Allies

There is no need for us to walk alone on our spiritual path. Energy is everywhere and if we align ourselves with that energy, we can utilize it and create.

There are many lifeforms throughout creation and even what we think of as empty space, isn't empty. We have many allies that are working with the light. Remember that one-third of the host of heaven is promoting our return to Source.

They are willing to assist us if we actively call upon them, but they cannot help unless we grant them permission. Humans have free will and no entities of the light are allowed to interfere with our decisions, even if we choose to remain unaware and separated from the truth of who we are.

Allies are often representatives of specific archetypal powers that hold the keys to that vibrational energy. They can direct potent energy to assist us with a solution to a problem, a healing, or a miracle.

A ritual is one way of aligning ourselves with the power of allies. It comes in many disguises: walking the labyrinth; Catholic Mass; sweat lodges; the medicine wheel, and the Wesak ceremony.

Ritual is designed to focus intent or to activate the will by stilling the mind. But if it is repeated too often, it could limit our vision because if we get locked into the limited purpose of the ritual, we have closed ourselves off to new possibilities. This is the error of thinking we already know what the mystery is about. This results in limited access to the unknown, meaning we become stuck where we are. Ritual can also become a crutch if we form a dependency on it.

In the beginning, the inclination is to use ritual and call upon the allies as though they are external to us. This is a good place to start, but eventually we need to do everything in our own name, rather than the ally's, for they are a part of us. With this internal approach, we aren't giving our power away or promoting separatism.

When we realize there is no power outside ourselves, our perception alters dramatically and we feel everything within ourselves. At that point, we can draw upon the energy of any of life's aspects at any time. We do this by turning inward and calling specific qualities to us, then we simply use our intent to direct the energy to a chosen circumstance. For example, if we wish to have the assistance of the wind to blow out a blockage in a person's chakra, then we merge with the wind element, become it, and feel ourselves blast through the blockage.

It is important to extend gratitude to the allies when they have assisted us. One way to do this is through offering a gift of thanks. This is a common practice among many Native American tribes. They offer things of value such as tobacco or cornmeal as an exchange for the gifts they have received. Find a way to show gratitude and it will strengthen your relationship with the allies.

We need to be careful whom we develop relationships with, since some would-be allies may have a hidden agenda. Be particularly cautious with spirits or beings from parallel realities that offer to feed us information in exchange for our energy. They may even call themselves by sacred names such as Chief Joseph, Mother Mary and others meaningful to us. It is a staggering temptation since these beings seem to be capable of increasing our knowledge[8]. This isn't a wise trade-off because they will continually deplete our energy. This can only occur if we see perception as something we receive from others. So the way to avoid encounters with these parasitic beings is to build a foundation of inner strength by knowing all power lies within. Guides that create a dependency are most frequently from these beings. The human right to be wrong is of paramount importance in our mission: to learn. A truly elevated ally won't usurp this right by telling us <u>what</u> to do or be. Higher beings are more concerned that we know <u>how</u> to do or be. Remember, what we have come to solve, not even God knows. That is why we were created. No one else can tell us what to do.

The Five Elements

The five elements are the earth (el), water (leem), air (om), fire (ka) and the ether. The ether can be called the substance of things hoped for. The ether isn't the void. It is a delicate substance that responds to thoughts coupled with emotion.

1. **Earth:** It is of great assistance when grounding is needed; when removing past trauma to repair distorted meridians; and for general healing. Scientists have found that the frequency emitted by the earth is the same frequency sporadically emitted by a healer's hands. Regular contact with her strengthens the immune and nervous systems in particular.
2. **Water:** Calcifications in the body are usually indicative of calcifications within our attitudes or world views. The conscious

---

8 In actuality, they are getting the information from us and are only telling us things we should have known if we had had enough inner silence to access it.

use of water can help release this and create fluidity of perception when relating to the world. Water is effective to remove debris picked up from others.

3. **Air:** It is used to clear the mind and as a vehicle to send intentions out for manifestation. Air assists in clearing social conditioning and world views that no longer serve us. It brings inspiration.

4. **Fire:** It is used in refining energy and aligning ourselves with our divine blueprint. Fire assists in purifying life issues and removing obstacles that stand in the way of our functioning from our highest perspective. It provides focus for ceremony and prayer. Its mystical qualities open doorways to the higher realms.

5. **Ether:** We tap into the ether when we consciously create an opening or vacuum for the universe to fill. We do this by presenting the blueprint and feeding it with our thoughts and emotions, until it is fulfilled.

Angelic Realm

To understand the role angels play, we have to divide the real from the unreal, the creator from the creation. In order to form its creation and study the unknown parts of its being, the creator divided Itself into seemingly separate components—its subpersonalities. If we understand the relationship of our subpersonalities, we understand a bit more about the Infinite. The One expressed as the many so its various components can relate, just the same way the nurturer comforts our inner child and the sage discerns when it is time for the warrior to protect our boundaries. So even within the realm of the Creator, division took place to be able to create its own projection, namely, creation.

In the realm of the Creator, it is the masculine or electrical (light) component that pushes each stage into the next. The angels are the "capacitors"[9] of God that work with the storage and discharge of light. A capacitor consists of positive, negative, and neutral components. Hence, the angelic realms are divided into a Trinity: angels promoting light, angels repressing light, and angels of neutrality.

The capacitor can be viewed as a jug held under a running tap that is filled and used for watering a potted plant. Its job is to receive, store and redirect where the water needs to go. In the same way, angels receive, store, and redirect light. Archangels have one more task. They step-down the frequency of the light before it is redirected. Even at the lowest levels of the angelic line of evolution—the smallest of devas and elementals (having as their task the forming of a blossom)—the same principle applies. They store light and release the charge so that light can be turned into matter.

Through prayers and the emotions of our heart, we create a sort of "magnetism" to pull in the flow of this light. That means it is impossible for the angels to ignore a sincere human request for assistance.

Being able to call forth angels through the desires of our hearts is one of the rare gifts of humanity. This communication isn't possible on all planets for it requires an emotional body. The angels of light have as their mandate, non-interference with the course of events as designed by mankind. They cannot offer assistance without our calling it forth.

Due to our limited human perspective, we often shun the angels of darkness. In rejecting their valuable contribution as the nega-

---

9 A device or being that stores energy until a means to release the charge is introduced.

tively charged component that permits light to flow, we perpetuate separation.

Angels are neither masculine nor feminine. However, their tasks lean toward the characteristics of one gender or the other as they represent aspects of the Divine.

Although there are many books listing the specific tasks and names of angels, you will find yourself forming a close relationship with a few. You will learn to recognize them by their vibration or fragrance, and sometimes they can be felt as a slight breath of air in your face.

The archangels that have closely worked with me are: **Raphael**, whom I encounter in the South, brings healing of both physical and emotional trauma and helps us to shed the pain of our past.

Michael comes from the West and brings protection for our light. He is often depicted with a sword for the simple reason that he is the one who separated the known from the unknown within Creation. In other words, he gathered all that was known about God's being to one place. We could then know that everything outside of that body of information is the unknown. Although this fact is often misunderstood, he was the one creating duality. His sword severs that which no longer serves us and cuts away scarring from our emotional bodies.

In the North, **Gabriel** provides balance, strength, fortitude and peace. It is essential after spurts of spiritual growth that there be an integrating period. After ecstatic states, these periods may feel almost empty and somewhat depressing, but we cannot constantly run on the high voltage of growth. There needs to be an out-breath and an in-breath. During these integrating periods, Gabriel provides balance and strength. At times when it seems as though the whole world is pulling us apart at the seams, Gabriel is the one who provides the fortitude to stand strong in the middle of our spiderweb.

Uriel brings new understanding. He is the one who assists us from one rung of the ladder of consciousness to the next. As we ascend, we access more and more light. He uses initiations to prepare us for these changes. Our nervous system, particularly, has to be adjusted to accommodate this influx of higher frequencies of light. He effortlessly transforms limited vision into expansive vision.

The Seven Powers

Understanding the different powers used to bring about the different creational phases allows us to align ourselves with these energies and create, heal, and uplift.

1. **The Power of Expansion:** This power represents the unfoldment of creation. It is that which becomes greater than its original state. This expanding power is an urge that compels all creations to be more than what they are at present. The Creator has formed these creations in order to gain more insights about the mystery of being, thereby becoming more luminous[10] with enhanced perception and increased power. Everything in existence seeks to become more of itself—even the Infinite.

    Examples of this include the continual expansion of creation in the form of a tube toris and the Big Bang that occurred to form individuation[11].

2. **The Power of Levitation:** This power is activated by the Three Ascension Attitudes. It manifests in a person who keeps his eyes fixed above the storm—who consistently focuses on the perfec-

---

10 Luminosity is increased light and light is information or perception. Increased perception yields increased power.

11 For more on this cosmology, reference "Journey into the Heart of God" Parts I-IV tape sets.

tion underlying appearances. A person living these attitudes adheres to the law of levitation and overcomes the law of gravity, thereby overcoming aging and death.

This is a life-giving energy in that it pulls lifeforce toward it. This is why people who use it through living the ascension attitudes, don't age. The law of gravity ages; the law of levitation youthens. An example is a plant growing upward, away from the earth.

3. **Form-Giving Power:** It is the power of sacred geometry forming the lines along which Spirit moves to create. An example of this is our mathematics, which is why it is sometime called Mathonian Power. It gives form to abstract concepts. It is like the metal gridwork of a building that holds the structure together.

4. **Expulsion Power:** This purifying power dispels blockages of dead energy and any filters that stand in the way of receiving light. It can be used to clear accumulated density from the environment or the body. As an example, this power is the propelling force when you send violet light through someone's body for purification purposes.

5. **Power of Inclusiveness:** It represents the primary purpose of creation itself—to include. This power transforms by embracing all things within itself. We utilize this power by including the unknown within the known by gathering the lessons within our experiences.

6. **Procreation Power:** It is that which recreates itself. An example of this is faith. It is simply a mindset that reproduces and manifests itself in outside circumstances. Another example is the ability to have offspring.

7. **Power of Resting:** This power defines a state of being in perfect equilibrium or rest. It is the result of an awareness that realizes its Oneness with all creation and that there is no point of

arrival or place to continue to expand to. It is represented in the cosmos by God Consciousness, and in the design of creation, by the pause between the out-breath and in-breath of God. When functioning with this power, all desires or agendas cease to be and action is taken from our larger identity as a being as vast as the cosmos. It is the most effortless way of influencing reality.

In a state of expanded awareness[12], we see with the eyes of God so we notice the perfection even within flaws. From this state, flaws disappear under our gaze. Any constriction of universal energy or flow is just an illusion. To remove these illusions we use the following technique: We become expanded attention and we just observe. We feel constrictions of energy but we don't judge. We don't resist or analyze. We simple observe with innocence. The constriction or flaws disappear before such an expanded, God-conscious gaze.

The Seven Lords in the Halls of Amenti

The Seven Lords govern different aspects of the earth's existence. Each lord is connected to a different chakra of the earth, which is connected to one of the seven rays of light or expressions of awareness. They reside in the Halls of Amenti, which is the life-force center of the earth in the fourth dimension. In the third dimension it is located under the surface of the earth directly below the Great Pyramid in Egypt.

Lords One and Two are lords of darkness who govern the underworld. The Seven Lords of light are known as Lords Three, Four, Five, Six, Seven, Eight and Nine.

12 Reference "Mystery School Healing Techniques" Part I tape set.

'How to' hint: If we desire to be in the presence of the lords of light, one technique is to envision an umbilical cord connected from the earth's lifeforce center to your bellybutton. Visualize your consciousness slipping through that cord and enter into Mother Earth's lifeforce center. The lords are there. They don't have form. Their presences are like balls of light.

If for some reason we don't find our entry into the Halls of Amenti, the incantation that opens the door is: MEKUT-EL-SHAB-EL HALE-ZUR-BEN-EL-ZABRUT ZIN-EFRIM-QUAR-EL.[13]

The Seven Lords[14]

Lord Three–Untanas: governs sending forth power. He holds the key of all hidden magic. He binds the souls of men by knowing whom death will hold. He helps regulate the opposition the "children of men" have to face.

Lord Four–Quertas: He frees the souls of men by knowing whom death will release. (Untanas binds and Quertas sets free, so these two work together.)

Lord Five–Chietal: governs sound. He holds the key to the word that resounds among men.

Lord Six–Goyana: governs the pathways of hidden mystical knowledge.

Lord Seven–Huertal: governs space. He holds the key of time and the time-space matrix.

Lord Eight–Semveta: governs the progress of things. He balances the journey of men since he knows the precise moment and order of unfoldment for everything.

Lord Nine–Ardal: governs chaos as it begins to merge into

---

13 "The Emerald Tablets of Thoth-the-Atlantean" by Doreal, pg. 80., Brotherhood of the White Temple, Casttle Rock, CO
14 Ibid., 35, 37-41

order. Darkness is chaos and light is order. He governs the point where the two converge. He creates form out of the formless.

If you sleep with the book "The Emerald Tablets of Thoth-the-Atlantean," on your chest for three nights, it is very likely that you will be taken out of body and shown the Emerald Tablets, or you will be taken into the Halls of Amenti. If you read its words, you will be altered because of the many levels of light it contains. There is a cadence to the words that activates your genetic codes.[15]

The Four Directions and the Medicine Wheel

Imagine creation as a reflection cast by the light of the Infinite shining through four different meshes that are superimposed over each other. These are lined up in front of the Infinite's light. The first mesh that formed is time. The second is space. The third is energy. The fourth is matter. All of the cosmos exists as a result of these four creational meshes. Therefore, everything in existence contains parts of these, although each will resonate to one mesh more than the others. That is why the Four Directions are helpful to categorize information because each direction represents one of the original meshes, or building blocks, of the Infinite. There are powerful archetypal energies associated with these directions. When we align ourselves with these energies they can assist us to accomplish certain tasks.

The center of the Medicine Wheel is the target position because it is the place of balance since it encompasses all directions. Therefore, it is the place of power. It is the same reason why we

---

15 For further techniques to connect with the Lords of Light reference "Internal Technology" Part I-II tape sets.

strive to be in the present moment because it is the center of the past and the future. When we are standing in the center of the Medicine Wheel, we can call forth any of the attributes from all the directions.

The South

The South is regarded as feminine in its attributes. The symbol for the South is a snake shedding its skin because this is where we shed the past. Shedding the past includes not defining ourselves by what we have been, but by who we are becoming. So like the snake, we shed our old skin to become new. When we have overcome the past, we are free of personal agendas and our emotional strings are no longer pulled.

As we shed the past, it is important to resolve our conflicts because unresolved issues weaken our energy fields and make us more susceptible to negative energy.

The yellow race and the physical body are in the South. That is why this race has been the one who has studied the meridians and acupuncture points of the body.

Our body provides physical signals to verify that we have found a spiritual truth. These body truths include: localized perspiration that has a lower salt content; a numbness around the lips; hairs standing up on the body; goosebumps; a vibration going through the body in waves; a tightening in the muscles; or we may find that breathing rhythms change.

It is the direction of the turtle. Its shell has 13 facets, which is the number of the joints in the body and the energetic plates of the earth. In the mythology of the Far East, the shell represented heaven and the square underside represented the earth, so it united heaven and earth.

The South is the direction for bone alignment.

The Four Directions

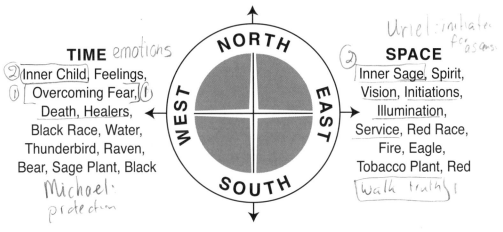

ENERGY

Inner Warrior, Ancestors,
Ascended Masters, Shamans,
Balance, Thought, Mastery of Mind,
White Race, Wind, Four-Legged Animals,
Most Birds, Sweetgrass Plant, White

TIME *emotions*

Inner Child, Feelings,
Overcoming Fear,
Death, Healers,
Black Race, Water,
Thunderbird, Raven,
Bear, Sage Plant, Black

SPACE

Inner Sage, Spirit,
Vision, Initiations,
Illumination,
Service, Red Race,
Fire, Eagle,
Tobacco Plant, Red

MATTER

Inner Nurturer, Healing of Past,
Physical Body, Body Truth, —
Yellow Race, Earth, Small Animals,
Turtle, Cedar Plant, Yellow

The West

She transmutes any negativity that we send to her. That is why this is the direction to release our fears. It is the direction of death, which is a purification rite.

The West is the direction of the emotions. The black race dwells there and their persona resonates with emotion.

It is the place of the rattle. It breaks up old energy, destructuring blockages, so a higher level of order can exist.

The bear resides in the West and is the totem energy that leads us out of the cave of the "dark night of the soul". The raven and the crow, which represent the path of power, also live there.

An obsidian stone can be used to cut away things that no longer serve us.

The North

In the North we learn to work with energy because we have the option to either align ourselves with it and create or alienate ourselves from it and destroy[16]. Conservation of energy is the objective and that means removing anything that drains our energy. It is where we learn to master the minds.

Our guides and ancestors come from the North. They teach us to live as a shaman, mystic, or master and how to work with power without loosing balance.

It is the direction of the majority of birds, and they represent thought. The birds of prey represent power. It is also the direction of the four-legged ones that represent balance.

The East

The East is the direction of illumination. It is where the sun

---

16 To learn impeccable ways of working with power, reference "Internal Technology" and "Mystery School Healing Techniques" tape sets.

comes up each day and lights our world, so we face the east as we face our inner illumination. It is where the awakening master receives vision or insights. It brings enlightenment, new beginnings, transformation, and initiations. (Initiations prepare the physical body to receive more light.)

By the time we get to the East, we know how to maintain our sacred space. Therefore, we are called upon to interact with the masses and live our truth in the clamor of the crowded cities. In other lifetimes, many of us were in the mystery schools. But this time it is important to come out of the monasteries and ashrams. We are to walk harmoniously between matter and Spirit.

It is the direction of the eagle and the red-tailed hawk, which represent vision.

Earth Heart Connection

Mother Earth is more than an ally, she is intimately connected with us through the heart.

The heart chakra is that which divides the lower three chakras from the upper three chakras. The lower three chakras are fed from Mother Earth, entering the body through the base of the spine into the bottom of the pranic[17] tube. The upper three chakras are fed from Father Sun, entering the body through the crown into the top of the pranic tube. These two energies meet in the heart chakra. This is the sacred, mystical marriage of light and love, or electrical and magnetic energy. Father Sun and Mother Earth's love-affair is consummated in the human heart.

---

17 The pranic tube is the size of the circle that forms when you place the tip of the thumb to the tip of the middle finger on the same hand. It is located in the middle of the body, extending from the crown to the perineum at the base of the spine. Unseen to the human eye, it nevertheless plays a vital part in the circuitry of the flow of energy in the body.

'How to' hint: Envision moving your lifeforce center from behind the bellybutton up to the heart. Connect your lifeforce center with an envisioned umbilical cord of light to Mother Earth's lifeforce center, which is a white ball of light in the Halls of Amenti. Connect your lifeforce center with another envisioned umbilical cord of light to Father Sun's lifeforce center. With each inhale, feel yourself draw up Mother Earth's energy from the bottom of your pranic tube. Simultaneously, draw down Father Sun's energy from the top of your pranic tube. Have the two energies meet in the heart. As you exhale, send love out from the heart in all directions.

When we allow this union to occur, it forms an energy field that becomes a tube toris. It connects to the body through the heart chakra. Through it, we are sending divine love out to all of creation, and the lifeforce of God returns to us, feeding the heart chakra from our back. It is a continual loop that feeds us energy so we no longer become tired. For this to occur, the seals of our chakras need to be broken so the energy can move freely. This is called having an open heart. When we have an open heart, it becomes a gateway for ascension. When we ascend, we travel through the heart chakra, but when we die, we exit through the crown chakra.

The words earth and heart have the same letters. The numerical value of each is eight, which in numerology represents "as above, so below." This means: we have what God has, and God has what we have; what happens to the earth, happens to us and vice versa. Therefore, our emotions effect the earth and the earth effects our emotions. That is why we see our level of consciousness reflected in nature: if our minds are polluted, nature is polluted; if our belief systems are full of old debris, the earth's surface is covered with old debris; if we are predatory, then there are predatory animals on

Marriage of Light and Love

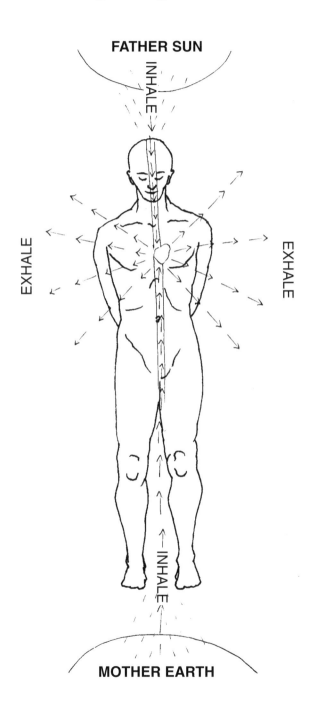

earth. The only time we are out of sync with the earth's energy is when we are in fear. Fear severs the connection by blocking the pranic tube at the second chakra.

The pineal gland[18] is a receiver of light, so we can use the pineal in various techniques to heal ourselves and the earth[19]. Mother Earth can heal us too. As a matter of fact, she is the ultimate healer. If we stay in touch with her in a loving way, we can receive her healing energies.

Ways the earth can heal you:
- If we have placed shields up to emotionally protect ourselves, it bends our energy lines inward. Lie on the ground and ask the earth to straighten your energy lines into the configuration of a masterful being's, i.e. radiating outward.
- If you have been around agitated, fear-based people, ask the earth to remove and transmute the negativity.
- If you are feeling ungrounded, ask the earth to help you remain in the body. Visualize roots extending from the bottom of your feet into the earth.

Balance of Masculine and Feminine Energies

Our feminine energies include: intuition, the creative process, receiving of non-cognitive information, giving birth to, nurturing. Our masculine energies include: the intellect, assertiveness, achieving, protection, and action.

The emotional-magnetic aspect is feminine and it includes our subpersonalities. This is the horizontal alignment. The mental-

18 The pineal gland is similar to an eyeball in that it receives light, via the crown chakra. It is located in the center of the head, two inches below the top of the skull, beneath what was the "soft spot" as an infant.
19 Reference "Healers of the West Wind: Sacred Keys to Healing Power" by Almine, December 2002

electrical aspect is masculine and it includes our three minds. This is the vertical alignment. When the horizontal and vertical alignments are in balance, they intersect through the heart. Then our lifeforce center moves up from the solar plexus, the place of logic, to the heart. The heart is the place of the interaction between feeling and cognition. This is an important step because when this alignment takes place, alchemical changes in the body are set in motion that are essential for ascension.

The split of the masculine and feminine energies not only exists between feeling vs cognition, but also between our left and right brain hemispheres. The right-brain is feminine and the left-brain is masculine. For ascension, we need to energetically merge the masculine and feminine. This means getting our left and right brains working together. When they are balanced, we activate Godmind.

Choose Life or Death

We need to determine whether it is a burden to be on earth, or whether it is the most extraordinary privilege any being has ever had. Do we wish to remain here, or not? Many of us haven't decided.

This planet isn't home for many of us and we want to return to our star-families, but this desire signals the body to release the death hormone. The only way to reverse that is through our attitudes because they determine whether our thymus, which is located in the heart area, will regenerate the cells or not.

Scientists have noticed an interesting thing that happens to a caterpillar when it forms a chrysalis (the stage prior to becoming a butterfly). An electrical impulse comes from the mid-brain that they can only describe as a "wave of determination." This sets in motion the life hormones that will change it into a butterfly.

For us to become an ascended master, we have to have our own wave of determination. It sets in motion a change in the endocrine system that causes the thymus to excrete the life hormone. We cannot accomplish this unless we choose life.

Light enters the pituitary gland through the crown chakra and the pituitary sends it down to the thyroid. The thyroid filters out the excess light that our body cannot hold. How much light we can hold depends on our attitudes. The thyroid says, "I'm only going to let a trickle in because he is still living in the past; or he is still looking at life as having good or evil; or he still believes in the contradiction that there are places where God is not." We cannot sustain these illusions and expect the full glory of Spirit to enter our cells. As long as we have limiting beliefs, the full potential of light won't be allowed to pass beyond our thymus, making it impossible to excrete the life hormone.

Deciding whether to remain on earth can begin as an infant since it is difficult for a high-dimensional baby to stay in the flesh. The body is uncomfortable so he may go to great lengths to get out of it, even by choosing a crib death.

When we choose life we start to excrete the life hormone and spiritual centers in the body begin to open. Our senses change. We start to see with extended vision. Even in darkness we see light being emitted from everything, including inanimate objects. The light will seem to be coming from inside the object or person. We start to hear the music of the spheres that fill all of existence. When people speak, we hear their heart's intent. Even the ground we stand on will appear, to our extended vision, as a sparkling gemstone.

Gold, myrrh, and frankincense help babies who are high-dimensional beings stay in the body. It may be placed around the crib.

CHAPTER FOUR

TWO ASCENSION METHODS

Filling the Cells With Light

Ascension can be achieved through the heart or through the mind.

The right-brain method of ascension occurs through pure feelings of love, praise or gratitude.

The left-brain method of ascension is accomplished through logic and mastering the mind. It is getting all the inner aspects in alignment so divine love can be felt.

The goal of both methods is to allow the cells to fill with light and to vibrate at the frequency of eternal love. The light is masculine (electrical) and the love is feminine (magnetic) and the balance of the two allows the glory of God Consciousness to come forth.

electrical= light + masculin
magnetic = love + feminine

Love is the core ingredient to both ascension methods but it comes through the ascension attitudes to those who are right-brain dominant. Left-brain oriented people are just as capable of divine love but they generally use logic and reasoning to get there. They access their love within by expanding their perception. This enables them to see behind the fear and release it. When fear dissolves, love remains.

Left-brain techniques have been taught in mystery schools all over the world for thousands of years. The right-brain method has essentially, been missing[20]. It is important that we reawaken the feminine method because earth is a planet of feminine orientation. Therefore, it is more natural for people on this planet to use a right-brain method.

The Right-Brain Method
Three Ascension Attitudes

Many people just feel. They aren't logically inclined so they don't question what they feel. They possess an inner sense of knowingness. These people function primarily from the right-brain and find it natural to be immersed in the Three Ascension Attitudes of love, praise and gratitude. This is the feminine approach.

If we continually live in the pure vibration of any one of these attitudes for a few months, it changes us from mortal to immortal. We become an ascended master in the flesh. This occurs because love, praise and gratitude are attitudes that indicate we have chosen

20 Reference "Mystery of Mysteries" tape set

life. These attitudes signal the pituitary gland to order the thymus to excrete the life hormone so our cells are continually renewed.

Praise

Of the right-brain options, the majority of people will ascend through praise. This is accomplished by living in complete devotion and by surrendering to the stillness within. Praise is seeing only the perfection. One outward expression of this is constantly singing to God. Another approach may be to use prayer.

Praise raises our eyes above the storm. It has no regard for fear or external circumstances. When Jesus Christ walked on the water, he didn't see the storm; he only saw the perfection. Peter was briefly able to walk on the water, then he focused on the storm—the appearances—and sank.

Praise has everything to do with awareness. If we start to become aware, we will find reasons to praise the Creator. Even when we experience a rough day and the pot has boiled over on the stove. The kids are screaming. Our husband hasn't come home and we suspect he is having an affair. The bills are late, again. Stop and take a deep breath and return to the present moment and realize: we are a spiritual being having a human experience; it is spring and the blossoms are in full bloom; a playful squirrel is staring at us from the tree outside the window; and there are meteorites shooting through the sky. Focus on the positive things so awareness can feed our appreciation.

When we live in constant praise light shines through the skin. We no longer walk in darkness for a soft glow literally lights our steps. This inner radiance becomes visible to others and it can be disconcerting to those we associate with, similar to the people being afraid when Moses came forth from Mt. Sinai bathed in the Christ light.

Some people use praise like a drug. They may go into worship for several days and sing to the glory of God. It is a high and they may be using it to escape reality. If that is the case, it has become a dysfunctional addiction. Continual praise is only healthy when the individual is balanced and incorporates it into the order of his daily life.

Gratitude

Gratitude is the next most common option for right-brain ascension. To feel grateful for all things we need to know that everything is in divine order—even the seemingly negative occurrences. This is when one understands that resistance is necessary for growth.

Before we can be grateful for all things, we need to see them as gifts, knowing it is an honor to undergo these challenges because it evolves God's awareness. If we live that attitude all so-called problems immediately dissolve. All hardships cease because we no longer have a need to draw painful circumstances into our life. We start to walk in grace.

Love

The most difficult right-brain option is through love because it requires that no fear be present. Fear is the desire to retreat and it blocks us from aligning ourselves with the intent of the universe, which is to enfold within itself—including all things. Love doesn't come on-line as a state of being until we align ourselves with this intent. When we do, love vibrates through the body's cells.

Praise and gratitude banish fear, therefore love follows these attitudes. However, faith in God and surrender to the Divine will are the components of devotion. Such devotion also melts fear and brings forth love. It is necessary for fear to be removed since it is the opposite of love—they cannot exist simultaneously.

Let us look at an example of a sheepherder in the Yucatan, Mexico. If he has continual praise for the stone-god in the mountain, it will enable him to ascend because it eventually dissolves fear. If the sheepherder is grateful for every circumstance in his life, including incidents when wolves slaughter his sheep and his son dies falling in a ravine, then he will ascend even if fear is present at first, for it will disappear. If he has no fear because he knows the stone-god will take care of him, love will come forth. If he is in a constant state of love for all things, then he will ascend.

We can raise our consciousness no matter what we worship by having love's vibration in our cells. This concept places the petty squabbling of churches over dogma into proper perspective.

We cultivate the Three Ascension Attitudes through focus. Start by thinking the most beautiful thoughts possible and focusing on what we have, rather than what we don't. Even if we can find only one thing to be grateful for and focus on it, our perception expands. Soon we will be able to see further and further behind the appearances. In this way, devotion enhances perception.

Each of the Three Ascension Attitudes represents a color (love is blue, praise is yellow, gratitude is red) and when they are combined, it makes white light: God's light. These are the white garments of the saints spoken of in the scriptures—the white light emanating from their skin.

The Left-Brain Method

If we are driven to understand who we are and insights hold great value, then we are left-brain oriented.

The primary goal of the left-brain method is to master the mind. It is to put the elements of the known in order, so we can access the unknown. The techniques used to master the mind can change the molecular structure and cause ascension to take place. Throughout the ages, these techniques have often been misunderstood and have given rise to deviance such as: deprivation of pleasures; living an austere life of seclusion in the monasteries; using mind-altering drugs; or putting the body through turmoil and torture. These extreme techniques may have provided some results but they aren't necessary. We only need to become free from limiting perception by using life as our tutor, and return to our natural state, which is divine love.

For practical purposes, the medicine wheel can be used as a schematic to work through our issues. The important thing to remember is the walk through the directions never ends. As we complete the wheel once, we go around again, moving up one level since the circular design of the wheel is actually an unending spiral. Each time we complete the East it forms a gateway. Then we are bumped up to the next wheel and begin in the South again.

The first spiral around the Medicine Wheel is the path of the initiate and its goal is self-empowerment. It deals with overcoming the past in the South, releasing fears in the West, learning to work with energy in the North and beginning to walk our truth among the masses in the East. Its task is to cut the strings of human programming.

The second spiral is the path of the adept. It involves reconnecting our subpersonalities. This is the emotional work dealing with the nurturer in the South, the inner child in the West, the adult/warrior/sexual persona in the North and the sage in the East.

The third spiral is the path of mastery. It is done from the center of the Medicine Wheel and it involves balancing the three minds.

You will notice as you work through these, that overcoming social conditioning is part of each spiral. It is actually a Medicine Wheel of its own, but for our purposes, we will include it with the others.

The first three spirals on the Medicine Wheel are what I refer to as Ascension Levels 1, 2, 3. They are the rudimentary steps of the left-brain ascension method. The best results will be achieved from working through the steps in the order presented because each is built on the foundation of the preceding one. If we skip a step, the structure weakens and may crumble.

When we master levels 1–3 it allows our Seven Bodies to be free from constrictions. For example, overcoming the past and releasing fears balances the universal flow of energy in the physical and etheric bodies. Reconnecting our subpersonalities balances the emotional body. Balancing the minds clears the mental body. We need these bodies open because the lower bodies, especially the mental body, keep us separate from the higher bodies, and until those are cleared, we cannot be one with our higher bodies— which is what ascension is.

Medicine Wheel – 1st Spiral: Initiate South

Overcoming the Past

Shedding the past frees us from rational expectations. Our expectations determine our future. For example, you love your partner but since every person you have ever loved has rejected you, you feel it isn't emotionally safe to get close to another person. This precipitates another failed relationship.

If we have these types of expectations, we are creating the past, over and over. Do we want to recreate our past in the future?

A good starting point is to redefine ourselves. Remember that we are not our experiences. We created the circumstances of our life to gain perspective. Whether Jane chooses to become a serial killer and John chooses to become a Lightworker—or any position in-between—it is all about learning the lessons. When we realize there is no path more valid than another, then judgment ceases towards others and ourselves.

This is important because the goal is to experience life with the innocence of a child.

Recapitulation

One method of overcoming the past is called recapitulation. It is the scrutiny of past occurrences that still control our behavior by causing us to have knee-jerk responses to people, events and beliefs. Recapitulation assists us to release debris and retrieve any parts of ourselves that became lost due to past trauma.

If we have any identity labels, a sense of self-importance, or if we are still judging people or events as good or bad, then we need to clear it.

Recapitulation can occur spontaneously, but more often than not, it requires effort. To make it easier, try placing it in categories such as year-by-year, family, spouses, sexual partners, friends, teachers, classmates, students, bosses, co-workers, etc. Sometimes we may receive snapshots of the past during the dreamstate, that is a signal that those events need to be released. It is also helpful if we can identify cyclical patterns in our life, then we can recapitulate a whole cycle and it releases all similar cycles. Consequently, as you review your life, be sure to watch for cycles within cycles.

This process occurs naturally at death. For several hours following death, our soul stays inside the energy field that surrounds the body (in the shape of an egg) and our whole life passes in front of us. As we witness this, we are able to see it from God's perspective, and as a result, our whole life is recapitulated. Then the soul passes through to the Spirit world and the energy field collapses upon itself.

Keys to Successful Recapitulation

- Remember how it appeared to us then (even through the eyes of a child if we were small)
- See the event through the eyes of the other participants. (A child may completely misunderstand an adult throwing him to the ground because of a perceived threat to his safety.)
- Relive the event, not just in our head, but in the heart, because we must feel it.
- Look behind the experiences and grasp what is really going on.

The following steps enable us to see behind appearances. This type of clarity yields strength because we no longer lose energy trying to make people and events relate to the world in a predetermined way. Consequently, we release the past and all the baggage associated with it.

Nine Steps of Releasing the Past

For any person or situation that still brings up painful emotions, ask these nine questions:

Please note that the first five questions assist us in seeing what is really going on. Use the intellect for this part because it was designed to help us discern what is behind surface appearances.

1. What is the lesson?

Look for the lesson that Spirit wishes us to embrace. For example, the lesson may be that we need to speak our truth. It could manifest as laryngitis, or someone might appear to mirror to us that we frequently suppress our voice. He or she may violate our boundaries to get our attention. We need to protect ourselves by voicing our truth that this behavior is unacceptable. Accepting the unacceptable isn't saintly, it is dysfunctional.

2. **What is the contract?**

Everyone who interacts with us has made an agreement, prior to this incarnation, to assist with our growth. They may have agreed to push us over the edge, and we may do likewise for them. Ask, "What is the contract that you and I are playing out?"

I have had several near death experiences and while in the spirit world, I was awe-struck by the extensive contracts people have with each other. It is with great love that many agreed to be a catalyst as perpetrators. When we are in balance, there is no growth so it is a signal to the universe to knock us out of balance so the lessons will continue. Thus, we pull relationships into our lives that test us in every way imaginable.

People don't like change and many go to great extremes to avoid it, even if it is a dysfunctional situation. The reason many dislike change is because they feel separated from Source. They believe that they are alone and completely cut off from nurturing by the Creator.

Understanding our contracts with others will help us accomplish what Christ said, "Judge not by appearances." What he meant was, when we are in the throes of tough experiences, don't look at them—look behind them.

3. **What is the role?**

Am I playing the victim? Am I playing the bad guy? Am I playing the teacher? Am I playing the student?

What role am I playing within this contract? Also, look at the role the other person is playing.

For example, we may have a tyrant in our life. It may be our spouse, mother, or boss. Once you establish that, see who you are in relation to that person's role.

Remember, we may change our role at any time because we create our reality.

4. **What is the mirror?**

We pull relationships into our life that do one of the following things: they mirror an aspect of who we are, what we have given away, what we still place judgment on, or what we haven't developed yet.

For example, if our innocence is gone, we may find ourselves intensely attracted to a young person. If we have given our integrity away, we might fall in love with a missionary who, in our eyes, represents integrity.

Another thing that can be mirrored, is that which we judge. If we have problems dealing with people who lie, then we are placing a judgment on them so we attract liars.

If a man isn't in touch with his feminine side, he might choose a woman who is overbalanced in her feminine to make him feel more complete. Later, he becomes frustrated because he cannot leave town for the weekend because there might be a leak in the water pipes and she wouldn't know how to handle the situation. These little irritations could build into resentment unless he sees that he deliberately chose her to mirror his underdeveloped feminine side.

5. **What is the gift?**

Every person we encounter has come to give us a gift and

receive one as well. This applies even with the most casual acquaintance.

Ask, "What gift am I supposed to give this person?" It may be something as simple as offering him the gift of unconditional love; or we may recognize something beautiful in him that nobody else has seen; or we may genuinely listen to a man and for the first time in years, he feels heard and understood.

Another time we may encounter a woman who reacts with bursts of anger and we have the opportunity to demonstrate our mastery of the situation.

'Note'–The last four questions deal with our attitudes surrounding the answers to the first five questions.

6. **Can I allow?**

This is the point of discerning what has to be allowed, what has to be changed, and finding the courage to act. Imagine yourself as the water in a river. If a rock is in front of you, are you going to stop or flow around the rock? We have masterfully created every situation in our life—even the rock—so can we just allow it to be there for this moment? Is this battle ours? A battle is only worth fighting if the stakes are worth having. If you have already learnt the lesson, no need to re-fight this battle.

7. **Can I accept?**

We cannot accept the painful things that happen to us unless we begin to see the perfection underlying the web of appearances.

A common belief is that we were placed on the wheel of reincarnation, suffering lifetime after lifetime, until we have lived enough lives to become perfect.

God created us perfectly with the ability to be a creator. Remember, thoughts plus feeling create activity. The heart is like a microphone so the stronger the emotions of our heart, the stronger the universe's response to manifest our desires. But the universe doesn't discriminate; it will manifest whatever we think—positive or negative. So it is important that we accept that we have co-created the situation, which removes any feelings of having things done "to" us.

8. **Can I release?**

To release is to let go of the energy surrounding the person or event. If we don't release, we keep it alive by feeding it energy through thoughts (sometimes subconsciously).

If we are in conflict with our partner, even if he or she has violated us in some way, the best thing to do is to walk through these steps and gain the insights. Then release it by changing focus and placing it onto something positive. That individual is like a vampire sucking our energy until we cut the cord that binds us. Every time we think of that person, send him or her blessings and the cord will be severed.

9. **Can I be grateful?**

If we have gone through these nine steps and can feel true gratitude for the insights gained, it raises consciousness. Gratitude is one of the Three Ascension Attitudes and is the culminating step. If we reach genuine gratitude, it assists us in connecting with our higher lightbodies and turning hardships into ascension tools.

If we have completed the first eight steps and don't feel gratitude, please go back and do them again.

When we look at the gifts, the mirrors, and the valuable lessons, we should be thankful for everything in our life. Even when the lessons are huge, such as being involved in a war, raped, or being an orphan, if we look at it from a higher perspective, it is a lesson or a gift. Even if we have suffered sexual abuse as a child, when we overcome it, we raise up the vibration of the earth because she has suffered the same. Also, when one of us overcomes, it is easier for the next person to do likewise.

Breathing Exercise to Overcome the Past

An additional assistance to overcoming the past is utilizing the breath. (The breath is very sacred because it is where spirit and matter meet.) For most of us, our past is complex so we may need to devote several days to this exercise, or spread it out over several weeks, releasing it bit by bit.

However, before we can release the past, we need to embrace it, which means going through the steps of recapitulation.

Breathing exercise: Pick one relationship, and start with your head completely turned to the right. I recommend that you place your tongue behind your upper teeth (see note below). As you turn your head 180 degrees to the left, blow out a negative aspect associated with that person. At the end of this step your head will be turned all the way to the left. As you move your head from the left to the right, inhale a positive insight you have gained about yourself as a result of that person. Identify another negative aspect of that relationship and repeat the process. Continue until there is nothing negative left to breathe out. We know we are finished when there is no emotional charge in us when thinking of this person.

'Note'–There is a repository of energy in the palate of the mouth. If you want to bring back memories from your dreamtime, fall asleep with your tongue behind the upper teeth. It provides extra energy so you can become a dreamcatcher, meaning you will remember your dreams and travels of the night. (A little pillow filled with mugwort will also assist. Place it under your pillow.)

For example, if we had a relationship with a partner who insulted and falsely accused us, and we felt we had to constantly defend ourselves, this would wear us down. Then one day we may have blown up in anger and terminated the relationship. Begin by turning your head all the way to the right and then exhale, releasing the frustration of continually having to defend yourself as you move your head to the left. Then inhale the insight you learned: a luminous being of light with a consciousness as vast as the cosmos, has nothing to defend because we are innocently having a human experience. During the next exhale, release the judgment surrounding the outburst of anger. During the next inhale, breathe in gratitude for having severed a relationship that was binding you because you weren't allowed to be yourself. Continue this exercise until every issue surrounding this relationship is cleared.

'How to' hint: Another method to add to the above technique of overcoming the past, is to go into the woods and gather twigs, having each twig represent a traumatic event in your life. Start a campfire, then position your body so you are facing the south and feed them, one-by-one into the fire. As you physically release the stick, release the person or event—including your pain and emotional attachment to it—and allow Spirit to transmute it. The smoke carries it away.

Relationships as Temples of Initiation

Our relationships are temples of initiation that bring to the surface things we haven't overcome, prompting a clearing down to the tiniest cobweb in the most remote corner of our internal closet. The people who are closest to us: our spouses, partners, immediate family, bosses, co-workers and friends, have contracts to push us into growth. That is why there is so much friction in intimate relationships.

People who are petty tyrants are gifts in disguise. Some shamanic traditions taught the initiate to find a petty tyrant if he didn't have one in his life. It was preferred that the person be in a position of control over a portion of his life and they be exposed to him or her on a regular basis.

Why are petty tyrants important? It takes practice to develop the ability to remain centered, and petty tyrants want to pull us out of our center. The petty tyrants will remain in our lives until we learn to release the past. Since these people are in our homes and work places, they are of extreme value in keeping our skills honed and to help us live impeccably every moment. In this regard, they prepare us for the unpredictable and the unpredictable prepares us for the unknown.

When we become God-realized we no longer need petty tyrants in our life, but until then, it is wise to recognize their value.

Four Categories of Petty Tyrants

The first category is comprised of the tyrants who live above the law and won't hesitate to destroy us. They will take any measures necessary to succeed, even unethical and unlawful acts, including physical violence.

For example, a woman's niece was kidnapped. Her sister's partner was the prime suspect. The woman had befriended the alleged perpetrator and wanted to stay in friendship with him in hopes of discovering a clue that could lead to legal prosecution. The man was a sorcerer and had managed to cover his tracks and read her thoughts, while masking his own.

Dealing with these tyrants can be life threatening because they are ruthless and you could be killed. Until you are fully God-realized and in your power, it isn't wise to associate with this type of person, so you may want to avoid this battle.

The second category of tyrants seeks to destroy us and are willing to take high risks but they won't resort to physical violence. These are the ones who use verbal abuse to attack at mental and emotional levels.

For example, if two men are competitive in business and one gains a seeming advantage. The subordinate man may start rumors in an attempt to ruin the other. He will go to great lengths to destroy his associate's reputation: lying to clients; entering inaccurate information on important paperwork; or reporting falsehoods to the FBI.

The third category of tyrants is unintegrated. They are the ones who present a friendly face yet perform incredibly hostile acts. These are the ones who don't take responsibility for their actions. They are generally steeped in fear. These people will be nice one minute and attack with rage the next. Their anger is like a disease that goes into remission until it thinks it is safe to come out. This type of tyrant is commonly found in the workplace and intimate relationships.

The fourth category of tyrants is the chronic naggers. They think nothing is right no matter what we do or don't do. This type of person is frequently found among family members and intimate relationships.

Freedom from Social Conditioning

The majority of what we believe and even who we think we are is a result of social conditioning. It comes in the form of identity labels and world views. It comes from our parents, society, and the culture we live in—the country, continent and the era. Within the social structure we have many groups telling us what to think and how to act: teachers, the media; entertainment industry; medical profession; financial institutions; scientists; governments; and religious organizations.

It is important to release the social beliefs we accept as truth and begin to access truth independently. When we overcome these limitations, we are operating from a position of an observer, and this yields strength.

Erasing Personal Identity

Labels are limitations. If we place labels on ourselves, others will believe them, and eventually, that is what we become.

The goal is to erase all personal identity. These labels include: I am a teacher; a healer; educated; the provider for my family; a conservative; a hippie; female; an American; human; or from a particular star family. For us to have any kind of persona is counter-productive. It pulls us back into ego. The goal is to retain personal awareness, but no labels.

Identity labels dictate a specific definition and role for the one who possesses them. It is a trap because people define themselves and others by these definitions. They think they know who we are, and oftentimes, even expect us to remain in that role. In this way labels become our prison bars.

A lot of energy is wasted trying to find our identity by comparing ourselves with others. For example, he is a male; therefore, I am a female. Often we pride ourselves in "humble" labels, but this is just another form of self-identity. As Lightworkers, we need to diligently remove labels so we can shed the illusion of self-importance. This requires watching every step we take to see where our beliefs are stemming from. For example, you are a teacher and a woman in the classroom does something you consider "inappropriate". The question must be asked, "What makes this action inappropriate?", and your answer might be that it is being disrespectful to the divinity of another. Based on this criterion, you then determine that she wasn't being disrespectful. So where did the feeling of inappropriateness come from? Did it stem from the label that you are a teacher and there is a certain protocol that should be followed?

Every time identity labels surface, stop and say, "I am all things, so why am I getting bogged down in these circumstances?" Then examine the label that is dictating your behavior.

When we become the All That Is, it is inclusive in nature. We become all things to all people as it fits the divine purpose. We may choose to wear different masks for different people. Each person may see us differently and that is appropriate because we don't have a need to prove anything to anyone. At that point, we stop taking things personally.

Erasing personal identity means we no longer define ourselves as anything. We are no longer encumbered by the weight of self-reflection, which is part of self-importance. When we eliminate identities and self-reflection, we become fluid and energy becomes more available to us.

Eliminating the labels enables us to access pure feeling and this enables us to access information from the unknown.

World Views

Most world views are based on limitation and that is the main reason why people don't achieve greatness. The world view says: we cannot build a flying machine; we cannot energetically heal ourselves; we cannot have world peace; and we cannot use the full capacity of our brain. It also dictates that one person is better than, or more important than, another.

In accepting world views, we are taking things at face value. Several spiritual masters have delivered the message "judge not by appearances". When we do, we fall into the trap of thinking we know and understand reality. This is arrogance because the majority of existence lies within the unknowable.

World views are overcome by not-doing. That means stepping out of the experience and observing it. We accomplish this by soaring above the situation so we can see the larger picture, like the perspective of the eagle flying high to assess all possibilities from all angles.

Using this technique of seeing with eagle vision allows us to observe the situation and carefully determine our response—whether to act or not. Initially it is a form of stalling that gives us time to become clear and safeguard the impeccability of our actions. It can be used to step out of a rut. For example, your grandfather is continually combative and rude to you, and over the years he has grown to expect you to be rude in return. Instead of reacting, just observe. If you choose to engage at all, let it be the unexpected. Give him a big hug and walk out the door. He will wonder all day about your response. Or, your mother routinely nags to draw you into an argument. Next time, step out of it and say, "Do you think so? I'll have to contemplate that one." Eventually not-doing becomes easy because one piece of the mind remains the objective observer, while another piece engages in action.

A crucial time to utilize not-doing is when we are in battle. In a state of emergency or surprise, the tendency is to lose our objectivity and fall back on old habits, yet that will only perpetuate past patterns.

With practice, not-doing leads to an inner stillness that slows mental activity and eventually helps stop the internal dialogue. Internal dialogue is the thoughts that maintain and reaffirm our world views. (This shouldn't be confused with the critical voice of the dysfunctional inner nurturer. That is the commentator.)

A master has no conditioned view of the world because he has stepped out of it. He has become humble enough to acknowledge that the majority of the universe is incomprehensible. He is open to new truths and questions everything: Who says we will catch a cold by going outside in the winter without a coat? Does fire have to be hot? Does water have to flow downhill? Does gravity have a constant hold on me? Can I hear people's thoughts?

If we only recognize fire's fourth-dimensional quality, which is light, we can wash our hands in it, just the same as in water. Fire's third-dimensional quality is heat and it burns most people because they have been programmed to think it is hot.

If we go outside in the winter without a coat and do catch a cold, it happened because we believed it would. It strengthened that belief when we stepped outside and opposed the cold, rather than letting it flow through us.

The Need to Know

People are addicted to the need to know. It is a result of fearing the unknown and attempting to control the environment by labeling things so we can rationalize away anything that doesn't fit into our existing views.

Society places a lot of pressure on us to know what is going on daily in the entire world, since it is readily available via satellite dishes and the Internet. The problem is that mainstream media sources are only feeding us more limited programming. Remember, all knowledge is within us. So take the information you receive (even this information) and discern for yourself what resonates as truth.

If a peer, student or client is pressuring you for an answer, say, "I'm not accessing that information right now. I will ask to receive it soon, and when I have the answer, I will tell you." It is okay to not know everything in every given moment. As a matter of fact, we reach a stage in the ascension process where Spirit clears the majority of knowledge and education we thought we had. We enter a state of knowing without thinking when we activate Godmind. Then we know what we need to at the right moment. When we don't need the information, the mind is so calm and clear that it seems as if all knowledge we had is gone. At that point we have been set free from the pressure to know and the need to be right about everything.

Medicine Wheel – 1st Spiral: Initiate West
Releasing Fears

Fear is the opposite of love. Love is the highest vibration in the universe. Everything that isn't in harmony with that vibration is a distortion of it. The distortion of fear is what gives the appearance that one part of life is more valid than another, that which we define as good or evil.

Our fears originate from incorrect perceptions perpetuated by social conditioning from the past. In fact, fears are emotions that masquerade as feelings. When we learn to see correctly, it releases the belief system associated with the fear and it dissolves.

When we know that we are the One expressing as many, it becomes clear that for us to fear another is to fear ourselves.

Those who wish to control us want us to live in fear. To become uncontrollable, we have to release our fears and expectations. We have to cease to need and know our being is our sustenance. When viewed from a higher perspective, all fears are irrational because love is all there is and all distortions are but an illusion. The illusions are in place due to a peculiarity of perception. We see life upside-down, the same way that images register on the retina. A fear is a universal truth turned upside-down, and to conquer it, we merely need to turn it right-side up.

If a fear surfaces, give it a voice and ask why it is scared. Fear may respond, "I'm scared of the maniac out there who is going to kill me." Then respond in a way to educate and soothe, "But who is this maniac? The maniac and I are One expressing as two individuals. For me to fear this maniac, I literally have to fear myself."

'How to' hint: After the fear states its case, then do these three steps.
- Call forth assistance from the Divine to remove the fear.
- Command the fear to leave.
- Issue the command, "Let there be light," so that the void that has been created will be filled again.

Removing fear is important because fear causes our energy lines to bend inward and that deprives us of power. Power is when our energy lines flow outward. When we release fear, we automatically become the vibration of love. This allows the lifeforce center to move up to the heart chakra and radiate love in all directions. At this point, we grasp the value of all beings and pour forth our love indiscriminately, regardless as to whether he or she is playing the role of light or undeveloped light.

One thing to be aware of is that the fear we are experiencing may not have originated from within us. It could be stemming from an outside source and we may be giving that vibration a home. This happens frequently, so always investigate the source. If it isn't your fear, banish it immediately. Then ask for the lesson as to why you allowed outside negativity to reside within you.

Death

The biggest fear most beings have is death, yet death is perpetuated by our thoughts. It is the creation of the surface mind that has spread through mass hypnosis, until the majority believes it to be real. Death and dying and decay have never been God's will. Eternal life is intended now—not after we die.

Death is optional. If we move into ascension our cells will become quickened and flooded with the Spirit of God. This is the second birth that is referred to in the Holy Bible. Death is a purification rite. We have made it a reoccurring part of life by our limiting thoughts and imperfection.

Many people associate death and rebirth with a wheel perpetuated by karma. The common belief surrounding karma is a misperception. Nothing in the universe is guilty of a wrongful act because everything is, and always has been, in divine order. If we see with limited vision, it causes a constriction in the etheric body and the energy becomes blocked. As a result, we have to create similar circumstances over and over, until we see clearly. Karma is a dispersal energy that wants to remove constrictions in the universal flow of energy. If we fill ourselves with light, there is no more karma.

We can think of death as a force that rolls against the sphere of light[21] that surrounds the body. Some ancient shamans called this force the Tumbler. When we are in harmony with all lifeforms, the Tumbler has a hard time causing aging and decay and death. Our sphere remains strong when it is constantly being fed by all of life, then the Tumbler cannot wear it down. If our sphere is weak, it cracks and folds upon itself, resembling the shape of an embryo, and we die. After death our lifeforce stays in the sphere of light anywhere from 3-72 hours and the spirit lingers near the body. When it completely crumbles and all lifeforce leaves, the spirit moves through to the third and fourth overtones of the fourth dimension.

It is our duty to overcome death. Jesus Christ said we are to "overcome all things, yea, even the last enemy," which is death. Jesus overcame death to show us that we can too.

Lack of Self-Worth

At the root of many problems is a lack of self-worth and the fear of not measuring up.

The sometimes subtle tyranny our parents hold over us needs to be severed. As an infant, we make the mistake of equating them with God. Then we see this parent-God as withdrawing his love from us when we don't do exactly as he says. That means we cannot depend on God to love us unconditionally. The churches that claimed God would withdraw His love when we didn't do what

---

21 Some ancient shamanic traditions call this sphere a luminous egg

He said, further reinforced this concept. This type of tyranny makes us believe we need to live up to other's expectations to survive or be loved.

This sets the stage for competition because we are afraid of not being good enough. This perpetuates the "every man for himself" mentality that has dominated society.

Another fallacy we bought into is that our body should look a certain way. For example, we may think our stomach is too big. Who told us it is better to have a flat stomach? Who set these guidelines? Learn to love and honor every piece of the body. It is the temple that houses the soul. It is sacred and perfect—just the way it is.

The concept of not measuring up is an illusion given by those who wish to control us. Not one of us has been short-changed. Our Higher Self gave us exactly what we need to fulfill our destiny.

The Fear of Destitution

The fear of destitution isn't determined by our income. It is due to a lack of understanding how we manifest abundance.

People who behave selfishly and with greed think they have to grab from others because nobody else is going to take care of them. They are overlooking the fact that they are in charge of their own sustenance.

We manifest continually, whether consciously or unconsciously. The preferred method is to do it consciously. Unaware people manifest by default and their limiting thoughts and dysfunctional pieces create a seeming lack of abundance. If we aren't having abundance, it is due to blocked perception. Perception attracts a similar vibration. Therefore, what we believe occurs. That is the basis of faith: a mindset reproduces itself. This is also the sixth

Creational Power.

Perfect creation is accomplished through the heart, using love. Thoughts fall into the reservoir of the heart and act upon "the substance of things hoped for." The substance of things hoped for is a delicate energy that is everywhere in existence, even in what we call the Void. (Technically there is no such thing as the Void because everything is within God's awareness.)

Emotion fuels manifestation. If our perception is one of victimhood, the emotion it creates is "I need" help or to be fixed. This creates more circumstances where we are going "to need" assistance from others.

The Five Laws of Abundance

Give that you may get–If you hoard money, you dam up the flow. Give money to the beggar in the street; a flower for a co-worker; a candle for yourself. As you give, the Infinite has to give too and it opens the sluices of supply.

Money is love–If someone charges us $1,000 for a bottle of water, we have to discern whether we wish to manifest the money to pay for it. Is it worth it to us? If it isn't, then simple release it, with no judgment or resentment.

Love is inclusive, so if we pretend money is love, it ripples outward until it includes all of creation. Therefore, all of creation's abundance is ours. It is a law that multiplies. On the other hand, if we view money as separate from us—something we need to get because we don't have any—it accentuates lack.

Sowing and reaping–There is always the option of working an extra job. However, sowing to reap is the least of the laws when our perception is locked on the result—to acquire money. There is nothing inappropriate about working one job or five, what matters is our attitude toward them. The higher law is: we don't sow that we may reap; we simple sow because we have seeds in our hands.

Bloom where you are planted–Create the mold by being specific about what we want[22] and then release it, so it may be filled. In the meantime, it doesn't matter that we are dishwashers and we want to be doctors. The key is to bloom where we are planted. We are in this job and the dishwashing is in front of us, so we dedicate that work to God. The gates of heaven will open for us if we take whatever we have as a task and perform it gloriously.

Gratitude is an expansive attitude–There is an ancient scripture that says, "Unto he who is grateful shall be added one hundred-fold, and he shall be made glorious." Gratitude increases the flow of abundance. When we say, "Thank you, Spirit," with genuine gratitude, it goes to the heart of the Divine. Our gratitude opens the windows of heaven and abundance pours through. When we send forth gratitude, the universe returns it by giving us more with which to be grateful. Gratitude stems from realizing that God sends us either lessons or gifts, and they are both the same.

If we find our only goal is making money, then we will be limited with that as our only exchange. It is a better plan to leave the universe in our debt. If we do so, the universe has to pay us, and it is going to do one of two things. Either it is going to pay us with money or with increased power and knowledge. Many healers who do their work for money only, become stuck at that level of ability. It is necessary in this society to have a flow of income, and charging for spiritual gifts is acceptable, as long as we realize that will be our reward. We may want to consider giving some of our spiritual gifts for free, in addition to our usual spiritual work, in order to keep the flow of money, or increased abilities, coming.

---

22 There is a difference between "want" and "need". A want is merely a preference, whereas a need is the result of seeing an outside thing, person or circumstance as essential for us to be complete.

If we leave the universe in our debt, it is always equalized. State the amount of money you want to flow to you each month and allow Spirit to deliver it from whomever or whatever means it finds. Have the faith to know that the money will find its way to you, so you can relax and freely give some of your gifts and abilities. If you do this lovingly, Spirit will reward you with increased knowledge and capabilities. The principle of tithing is based upon this law.

This style of manifesting utilizes the creating of a vacuum. For example, if you need a pair of pantyhose. Say, "God, please help me get the pantyhose," and open the vacuum within by creating the want. When you do that, the universe will rush in to fill it. The next day, someone will hand you a pair of pantyhose.

This isn't focusing on lack. It is establishing a desire with hopeful anticipation. In I Corinthians 13 it says, "now shall remain faith, hope and charity." The principle of hope is generally misunderstood. It is a form of waiting for a mold we have created to be filled. Firstly, it is important not to come from need, but from want. It is merely stating our preference. Once you are clear with your intent, state what you want in great detail. If we don't get the pantyhose, that is fine. We will wear the shoes without them.

While we wait with a knowingness that it will manifest, act as if we already have it. Visualize yourself using this object or personal characteristic with great love, stating how wonderful it is and how grateful you are to have it. This technique is highly effective because like attracts like.

Declaring the desire, fueling it with emotion, and giving birth to the creation are right-brain, feminine aspects of manifesting. It needs to be balanced with the left-brain, masculine aspects of discipline and structure, which is keeping the focus, applying will, learning to make money grow and setting boundaries with money so we don't leak this crystallized form of energy. This is stewardship.

For example, a woman may effortlessly manifest money. Consequently, she may adhere to the philosophy that if somebody genuinely needs money, she gives it. She doesn't worry that she has just given away the grocery and gas money because she knows she can manifest more. So she gives and gives. Eventually, she will find herself in debt because the flow needs to be balanced with management. This is to mirror that she needs to develop the skill of harnessing money and become a good steward.

According to the rules of good stewardship, we have to consider whether giving money to solve other's money problems is being co-dependent. Beyond that, she may be seeing them as victims and not honoring the fact that they created this situation to learn a lesson. Jesus Christ didn't hand out money, but he did multiply the bread and fishes to set the groundwork so others could do likewise.

We need to make sure our money, which is universal energy, flows freely, but at the same time, we have to be careful not to feed another's self-image of lack.

Another way people perpetuate the image of lack is by asking, "Can I afford this?" That implies a mindset that says, "I am limited." Although I am not suggesting we buy a million-dollar yacht if our annual income is $25,000, it does mean that we spend within our general budget without worrying about every dime of every purchase. The goal is that the energy surrounding the purchase be one of abundance and gratitude—knowing the money is there and when those dollars are spent, more will rush in to fill the vacuum.

Make sure your buying isn't due to un-recapitulated areas in your life. For example, you had a favorite red coat as a child and your mother gave it to another child who was cold and didn't own a coat. As an adult, you now buy two red coats for your daughter.

If this purchase reawakens pleasant memories of how glorious you felt in your red coat, that is fine. If it stems from a buried resentment or a compensatory motive, it is causing you to react and you may wish to release it.

The payoff for taking charge of our own sustenance is that we cease to need, and when we cease to need, we become uncontrollable.

Medicine Wheel – 1st Spiral: Initiate North

In the North we learn to conserve energy. This is important because personal power, as well as consciousness, is determined by how much energy we can hold.

All initial energy goes to access left-brain and only surplus energy goes to access right-brain. When we conserve energy through bringing order to the thoughts of left-brain, we can access right-brain and it is the right-brain that accesses the unknown, which is 11/12ths of what can be known by man.

Choose Your Battles Wisely

Losing energy is losing power, so carefully choose your battles. The majority of battles aren't worth fighting because the results aren't worth having. The only thing worth fighting is the illusions that hide clarity of perception. Don't view anything as a problem, but rather see them as challenges that potentially hold the gift of power.

The decision to engage in an outer battle is done from a place of inner stillness with no personal agenda. It is a simple law that whatever we send out, comes back. If we intend to harm, we open ourselves to receiving harm. The only time it is appropriate to curtail a plan or bind another is when specifically instructed by Spirit. We won't be asked to do this unless we are free of personal agendas and not attached to outcome.

The valid battles are always to release the mystery of our beingness, it may only appear to be with another. When faced with a challenge, analyze whether this battle has an underlying lesson that you need to extract. If so, does it need to be fought now? The key is being able to cut through the drama to what is really going on. Then we can determine whether a response is needed. If the reward isn't worth the output of energy, we don't enter the battle.

If we haven't developed enough skill, it would be inappropriate and possibly dangerous to take on certain tyrants. The best choice may be to turn away. Making the decision to engage is like being an ocean surfer: we see which waves are ours and which are not; we don't ride every wave.

The challenge is seeing behind the appearances of the problems that arise in our life. When we see the lesson that the problem brings, it alters our perception and perception yields power.

Things that Drain Energy

Identifying debilitating patterns that cause energy leaks is crucial. We find these patterns by watching for knee-jerk reactions. Following are some potential problem areas to check.

Relationships

Relationships that no longer hold a lesson can drain energy so we need to assess which ones are genuinely serving us. We are either expanding or contracting at all times. If someone makes us contract, discern whether he or she has a lesson. If not, release the relationship and move on. If they do have a lesson to offer, the highest choice is to welcome the challenge because if we ignore it, it will manifest in another relationship. Have you noticed repetitive patterns in relationships? The only way to break the pattern is to embrace the insights the challenges yield. Co-dependent relationships cause a huge loss of energy. This is when we are trying to control others or trying to please them. We attempt to control others when we fear change and are desperately trying to make someone fit into our world view. We attempt to please others when we allow their expectations to determine our actions. An example is every time our mother comes over, we work extra hard because the little girl inside wants approval.

Not only do we desire to control others and the environment, but we spend a lot of time trying to 'relate to' events and people. For example, if we see a toy in a garage sale, we may say, "I had one of those." If we hear a song we say, "I wish I could sing beautifully," or "I can sing better than he can." This habit reinforces the separatism of the ego.

If we have gained our lessons and set boundaries with difficult people in our lives, and they continue to breach our boundaries, it is appropriate to release these people—even bloodline family members. It is okay to choose a new family that vibrates harmoniously with who we are. Others are waiting to play the role of being our mother, father, sibling or grandparent, who will do so from a loving and healthy position.

Ordinary Things

Everyday items and interactions can adversely interfere with our energy fields and physiology. The following things weaken our auric field and make it permeable by lower-level beings or negative energy:

- Alcohol, drugs, nicotine, excessive caffeine
- Electric blankets, radio-towers and fans
- Microwaves, TVs and cellular phones
- Sex with a partner who vibrates at a lower energetic level
- Unresolved emotional and mental conflicts

Drugs

Drugs prevent us from feeling pain, but they also prevent us from accessing light. People who use drugs, including dental narcotics and marijuana, have a thick grayish mucous in their etheric body that hangs around the head and over the heart. Heavy drugs can also cause distortions in the mental bodies.

People who have used marijuana a long time or heavy-duty drugs even a few times, have overactive adrenal glands. This pushes them into a constant state of anxiety because the body interprets the spurts of adrenaline as a response to fear. They then use more drugs to calm themselves. Continued drug abuse causes the adrenal system to become dominant, when the goal is to have the pituitary system be dominant because that is the natural condition when we are in balance. A fully functioning pituitary gland provides us with visions and insight.

Noise

Noise pulls us out of the present moment and pushes us into a state of imbalance. It is essential that we have silence. When we are in a place of silence the heart chakra opens. It also enables us to connect with the primordial earth (a time prior to manmade noises) which is very healing.

Noise is increasing ten-fold every 20 years. It has become so insidious that many people aren't aware that they are constantly bombarded. Take note of your environment and see if you can acquire more silence. Check your refrigerator and the heating system. Are fans running? Does your wristwatch beep? Do you allow the dog to bark constantly? Does your computer beep or talk to you? Does the car signal you with jingles and blares?

Those disconnected from their subpersonalities cannot stand silence. They enter a room or get in the car and immediately turn on the TV, radio, or stereo. They go into the wilderness and take along music, claiming they don't want to become bored. In actuality, they want a distraction so they don't have to face the emptiness inside that silence might reveal.

Surprise

Surprise drains energy. The unexpected and the unknown can pull us out of balance, so we need to approach things with equanimity. When presented with the unexpected, role-play and act "as if" we already know, even when baffled. We merely form a hypothesis stating, "This might be true," and then we wait. This is a stalling technique to gain the time to center ourselves, see behind the appearances, and discern whether action is needed. This is developing an attitude that enables us to constantly guard our energy so we are less likely to be preyed upon by those who wish to steal it. Everything requires energy, so it is the most sought after commodity in the universe.

Words

We cannot define ourselves by who we have been. We must define ourselves by who we are becoming, and we are becoming masters of light. Consequently, we cannot insult the god and goddess within by saying derogatory things: I am poor at math; I am scared of mice; I am ugly; or I am terrible with managing money. That was yesterday—redefine yourself today. All knowledge is within us. All talents are within us. All beauty. All power. Watch your words and only speak those that reflect who you are. (A good rule is to never follow the words "I am" with anything negative—including the word "sorry".)

Self-Reflection

If we are obsessing about the what, why and how of every thought and action, we are indulging ourselves. This bends the energy lines inward and places us in a weakened state. Obsessing about the questions brings the baggage of the past moment into this moment, meaning we aren't traveling lightly enough to do the powerful work of transformation. For example, if you are traveling 70 mph in bumper-to bumper rush-hour traffic and a truck attempts to sideswipe your car, you jerk the steering wheel to the left and barely squeeze between two automobiles in the fast lane. The few seconds following the incident are critically important. If you fall into self-reflection and say, "Wow, that could have been a serious accident. That man was trying to kill me!" and continue to mull it over, you are losing too much energy. Therefore, you won't be prepared for the next moment. Twenty seconds later, he does it again. Are you centered and ready to respond masterfully, or are you still shaken and feeling afraid? Which state you are in may determine whether you survive the second attempt.

Self-reflection includes feeling sorry for ourselves: nobody pays any attention to me; my boss doesn't know how valuable I am; and nobody understands me. The other aspect is giving ourselves labels and comparing ourselves to others. With comparisons, if we say we are less than another, it is worshipping another's arrogance.

We straighten energy lines by embracing life with awareness in the moment. This causes the energy around our bodies to radiate outward. The self-centered person constantly engaged in self-reflection, bends these energy lines inward. This causes decay and eventual death.

A Master is Self-Referring

A master is self-referring for his approval, so he doesn't react to other's words or actions. He knows not to expect approval from the majority. Society lives by tradition and world views. In fact, society is a society because of its attachment to those world views. A master has released these views and so society rejects him.

Conditioned Life vs Unconditioned Life

The "conditioned life" cannot grow beyond certain limits because it is imprisoned by world views and social conditioning. It is better to strive for an "unconditioned life" because it conserves energy. This energy is now available to us and can be used to access the non-cognitive information of right-brain, which reveals the unknown, and eventually, the unknowable.

Conditioned Life

- Has fixed expectations as to what life should be
- Anticipates and attempts to determine the future
- Is trapped by defending their world view's validity
- Believes their life path is determined by social conditioning. They pretend to search for truth when in actuality they are searching for that which further reinforces their existing beliefs.
- Depends on predetermined causes and results
- Has a fossilized consciousness that doesn't flow. Rigid consciousness blocks energy.
- Takes a great deal of energy to sustain because it is based on illusion
- Accesses reality through world views and social conditioning, so

life is full of ruts and habits

Unconditioned Life

• Accepts life moment by moment as it comes, without expectations
• Allows the future to come to them, realizing that a planned future is a closed one.
• Accepts the validity of all paths
• Realizes their life path is determined by working together with the Higher Self. God's will becomes their will.
• Is spontaneous and innovative
• Possesses a fluid consciousness that draws in energy by becoming new each moment
• Doesn't require much energy to sustain, therefore, people stay young and rejuvenated
• Accesses reality through insights gained from experiences, so life reveals itself anew every moment

Medicine Wheel – 1st Spiral: Initiate East

In the East we begin to walk our talk among the masses. We offer ourselves in service to Spirit and it is service from a position of fullness. We are no longer serving for ego-based reasons, such as wanting to be needed or saving others we see as victims.

The East is the direction of vision. By the time we get there, our future isn't being determined by our past, our rational fears are gone and we know how to conserve energy so others aren't able to knock us out of our center of power. At this point our service is pure and we aren't identifying with it at all, for we know the biggest contribution is our inner state of being.

We see life symbolically. For example, someone has stolen money from us, so we look for the symbolism behind the occurrence. It doesn't necessarily mean we have directly stolen from another, but we ask ourselves how we may have inadvertently stolen from another or ourselves. Are we stealing our own power by allowing another person to control us? Are we underpaying an employee who is willingly working beyond his duties? Are we cheating ourselves out of our rightful abundance by not taking responsibility for our wealth?

Medicine Wheel – 2nd Spiral: Adept

Connecting the Subpersonalities

Within each of us are a nurturer, child, adult (includes the sexual persona and warrior), and a sage. When these subpersonalities are connected and allowed expression, we have a happy, stable, inner family. Our inner family enables us to love and fulfill ourselves so the pain of separation abates. The resulting self-sufficiency makes us uncontrollable and unable to be manipulated by others.

The subpersonalities are the emotional components and acquiring balance between them is crucial to stop co-dependent patterns with others. If we overlook this, we could mistakenly use our personal power to manipulate others to fill the gaps that we should be filling. When the inner family is connected we are never alone so we are secure within ourselves. This means we are no longer emotionally dependent on others, so we stop reacting and start responding to people and circumstances.

It is important to keep our subpersonalities happy, whole and expressed, but many Lightworkers tend to overlook this. They are too busy and when time is devoted to spiritual practices, they prefer to study advanced esoteric information. But before we can become a powerful master of light, we must be present in the moment, and the only way to be fully present is by having the subpersonalities hooked up. (We aren't going anywhere without our inner family!)

Balancing the subpersonalities is essential prior to balancing the minds. It represents the horizontal alignment that precedes the vertical alignment. In ancient Egypt, the initiate going through the side temples to reconnect the subpersonalities prior to entering the Great Pyramid reflected this.

We were deliberately disconnected from our subpersonalities by the undeveloped light as a means of control because if we became scattered and dysfunctional, we are powerless.

When the subpersonalities are expressed, we have a self-supporting system that allows us to be in the moment—the place of power. Reconnecting the subpersonalities is the quickest way to reach a state of joy. At that point we are clear of agendas and cease to need so we can freely give. This is when miracles begin to happen.

Adept South–The Inner Nurturer

The nurturer is the parent of our inner child. It offers comfort and support and sets healthy boundaries for the inner child to function within. It makes sure the inner child is given time to play and express itself. When we parent ourselves, we are no longer controllable by parental figures, and this includes authoritative institutions.

The dysfunctional nurturer nurtures everybody else—forsaking the self. The child is ignored because the nurturer isn't present. It also sets itself up as a judge.

If we didn't have good parents, we can become them for ourselves. We can heal childhood injustices and abuse by providing our inner child a happy childhood now. We also do this by healing our timeline.

> **'How to' hint:** Imagine yourself standing in the center of a figure eight with the future being the loop in front of you and the past being the loop behind you. As described earlier, the intersecting point is at the lifeforce center. To access the past, visualize yourself walking the loop behind you, counterclockwise, beginning with this year and rolling time backward. Stop when you reach the year you wish to alter. Visualize yourself being the ideal parent for your inner child. Fill in as many details as possible: say loving, comforting and inspirational things; play together; watch movies together; and talk your child through difficult times. Return to the present when you wish, but continue visiting the child until you feel it is strong enough to cope.

Physically do as many things as possible that were missing from your childhood. For example, a woman had alcoholic parents and as a child she had to be the adult of the family. Consequently, she never got to play. She had always dreamed of having a tea party, so a friend bought her two beautiful porcelain dolls and this adult woman now has tea parties. It is never too late to have a great childhood!

It is also never too late to have a good parent or to become one for your physical children. Use the principle of the timeline and go back and change how you have raised your children. Fill in pleasant memories as if they happened. If the child is perceptive, he or she will notice the energy shift. For instance, if you go back and allow your child full expression rather than telling him to be quiet, you may discover that henceforth, your child has found his voice.

When the nurturer goes awry and becomes a controlling parent it becomes judgmental of our words, actions, or appearance. Frequently, he or she is the critical perfectionist who comes along behind you to redo or undo what you have done, claiming, "You never do anything right."

When we are balanced, we may reach a point where we choose to do things as beautifully and perfectly as possible. Then our labor is an act to honor the Divine within. Nature takes thousands of years to perfect the beauty of a flower, so I can take a few seconds longer to make my bed beautifully, or remove dust from the dining room table, or serve my guests with crystal and china.

Adept West–The Inner Child

The inner child plays and feels. He or she lives innocently and spontaneously.

This child is connected to the web of humanity around the planet. We cannot disconnect from mortality unless we go through the child. That means the inner child needs to be parented by us since even the best parenting is usually faulty since it is done conditionally: if you don't do what I say, I will punish you; this is right and that is wrong; and you must be socially acceptable or be rejected. When the inner child is nurtured and loved by us, it becomes secure and happy. At that point the earth releases us from the web of mortality, and we can become immortal masters.

The dysfunctional child's energy lines bend inward, by saying, "I need. I want. Look at me." He strives to receive attention because he feeds on the energy that focus provides.

The happy child is the joyous being who passionately relishes the moment. Have you noticed how a child may be crying one minute, and the next, a butterfly may flicker by and he chases it with great enthusiasm? That is the healthy inner child. The last minute is past; the next minute isn't here. We only have now.

The innocence, spontaneity and unconditional love of the inner child keeps energy flowing into the lifeforce center. This freedom of expression allows the inner child to access pure feelings, which is a non-cognitive way of accessing information.

A word of caution when using any divination tools; be sure it is your Higher Self and not the inner child. The inner child won't lie, but he or she loves to play tricks on us.

Adept North–The Inner Adult/Sexual Self/Warrior

We aren't ready to have an intimate relationship with another until we have one with ourselves. We need to know our inner adult. Many people don't know what they like. They seem to have lost touch with that part of themselves. When asked what they like, their response is about what used to be. "I used to like riding a bicycle when I was a teenager," or "the greatest thing in my childhood was camping," or "I read a lot when I was younger."

It is important to have a passionate relationship with our adult. Take yourself out on a date for a candlelight dinner, a movie, a walk in the forest, attend an outdoor concert, or go to the park and sketch or paint. Also, pamper yourself. Take an hour-long bubble bath with candles and soothing music. Get a therapeutic massage.

Sit under a shade tree by a creek or fountain.

Do whatever makes your heart sing. Living passionately pushes back the density. If we spend all our time doing work outside ourselves—even if it is work that may be making the world a better place—the density will eventually suffocate us.

We also need to approve of our sexual self. Many people keep their sexual personas hidden in the closet since they don't understand them. Our sexual desires and beliefs can seem odd because the blueprints formed very early in our psyche. For example, something quite innocent may have aroused a young boy, such as an adult stroking his hair. He may thereafter, associate someone touching his hair as being sexual. As an adult he may avoid touching other adults and his children on the head.

We have been deliberately disconnected from our sexuality because it contains enormous power and has the capability of kicking us into other dimensions. So we were made to feel guilty towards sexual behavior. This was done through social proprieties—rules of what is appropriate and what isn't. To distinguish between right and wrong choices regarding sexuality, consider this: the highest choice is the one that most fully reflects who we are, all-knowing, all-powerful, luminous beings of light. A further consideration is that anything that harms another simply cannot be acceptable.

The function of the inner warrior is to protect our boundaries and fight anything within that would rob us of power. It guards our thoughts with merciless persistence. The warrior becomes dysfunctional when fighting circumstances in the external world, not realizing that we strengthen that which we oppose and we empower that which we focus on.

Adept East–The Inner Sage

The duty of the inner sage is to use discernment to keep the other subpersonalities aligned.

For example, if the nurturer turns into a critical parent, the sage steps in and says, "It isn't your job to judge, but only to love. The child is needing you so merely love him." Perhaps, in an intimate relationship, the other person may be having a relationship with your needy inner child because your inner adult isn't hooked up. Then the sage says, "Become that child's parent so she feels safe. Then honor your adult self so you can have a wholesome relationship."

When the inner sage is hooked up, it looks for anything that is left in the deeper levels of the subconscious that still needs to be recapitulated. This includes events from other lifetimes. The sage watches the interaction of his family members to see what needs to be flushed out using the tools presented in the initiate level. For example, if the warrior won't put his weapons down, even though the nurturer declared it is time to rest, the sage will have to explain why fighting is no longer required and why exerting further energy is a waste.

The sage becomes dysfunctional when he looks for truth outside himself. The many multitudes of churches that have sprung up through the ages can attest to man's search for the divine outside of himself and through designated intermediaries.

Another dysfunction of the sage is when discernment becomes judgment. We separate out dissimilar components, in whatever form they represent themselves, for the sake of being able to apply discernment. However, if we start placing a value on those discernments, then it becomes a judgment.

It happens frequently that one subpersonality usurps the role of another. For example, if the nurturer and adult aren't present the child becomes homeless and scared. This results in the child appearing at awkward moments. It may show up bewildered or hysterical in a state of emergency, when it is appropriate for the warrior and sage to handle the situation. Another example is when a man's child may appear when his sexual self should, so he is joking when it is more appropriate to be intimate with his partner. If the child takes over the duties of the warrior, it nags and causes havoc.

The ability of the sage to use discernment doesn't come into place until the other three subpersonalities are balanced. That is why there is an order to the steps of overcoming and releasing.

Gathering Truths

Each of the subpersonalities accesses truth in a unique way. The nurturer gathers it through body truth because it is in tune to the body's needs, such as when it is tired, needs cleaning, healing or to be pampered. The child uses feelings as its guide. The adult uses the intellect. The warrior uses instinct. The sage uses inner knowing.

Here is an example of how you can use the subpersonalities in making a decision: It is tax time and you owe the government $5,000 that you currently don't have. You decide to hold a board meeting and call forth your subpersonalities to help you make the best decision on how to come up with the extra funds.

The nurturer is the first to speak. He knows the law of giving, so he says, "Give that you may receive more fully."

The inner child raises his hand. He knows the law of abundance that declares money as a denser manifestation of love, so he thinks he has the solution. When you call upon him, he says, "We'll play a game and pretend that money is love. I know taxman is difficult to love, but he is the collective consciousness of this country that we placed there. He is saying, 'I don't feel very loveable, therefore, I need all the love from you that I can get.' Are you going to refuse to share your love and keep it all for yourself? Let's give taxman the extra love."

Next is the inner adult. He knows the law of sowing and reaping, so he suggests taking a second job. He admits, "It is going to be hard. I won't see the kids as often and I'll be tired, but it will help cover these bills that aren't getting paid."

The inner warrior stands up and declares, "I'll give you the strength, because I am your second wind. I will support you through this tough time of working an extra job."

Then the sexual self says, "I know how to get what you want, you ask for it and while waiting, you focus on what's in front of you."

On the east side of the table, sits the sage. He knows the power behind the law of gratitude, so he suggests, "Pay your bills with gratitude. We know there is abuse of the tax money but don't focus on it. Send your money with the intent that wherever it goes, it will positively change the world. Write each check with gratitude, knowing it will increase the flow, returning to you a hundredfold."

Medicine Wheel – 3rd Spiral: Mastery

Uniting the Three Minds

We have three minds: the subconscious mind, surface mind and Godmind. The goal is to unite them so they function harmoniously, allowing the Godmind to come forth.

The mastery level is done from the center of the Medicine

Three Minds

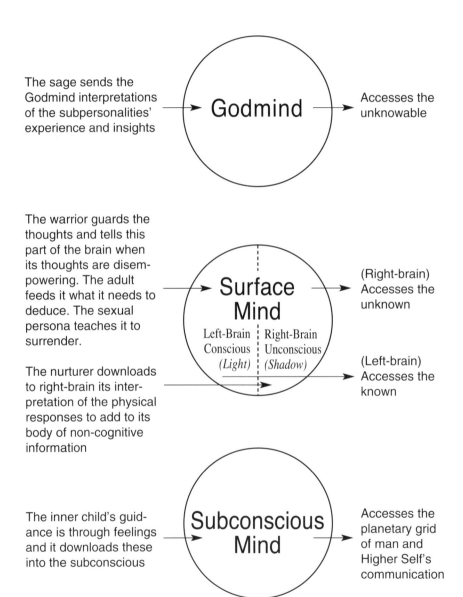

The sage sends the Godmind interpretations of the subpersonalities' experience and insights

Godmind

Accesses the unknowable

The warrior guards the thoughts and tells this part of the brain when its thoughts are disempowering. The adult feeds it what it needs to deduce. The sexual persona teaches it to surrender.

The nurturer downloads to right-brain its interpretation of the physical responses to add to its body of non-cognitive information

Surface Mind

Left-Brain | Right-Brain
Conscious | Unconscious
(Light) | *(Shadow)*

(Right-brain) Accesses the unknown

(Left-brain) Accesses the known

The inner child's guidance is through feelings and it downloads these into the subconscious

Subconscious Mind

Accesses the planetary grid of man and Higher Self's communication

Wheel. This spiral begins from below, where we clear out the sub-conscious mind. The second step is in the middle, where we bring left and right brains together in the surface mind. The third step is above, where we activate Godmind, which is the place where we have access to all knowledge and information.

A major shift occurs when the two halves of the surface mind are brought into balance. At that point the left-brain is in its proper place so the conscious mind is no longer serving as a barrier between the lower bodies and higher bodies. This allows access to the three higher bodies so the effortless knowing of Godmind can take place.

When this occurs, we fill with light. The heart center signals the cellular structure to alter. The nucleus of the cell, which was small and round with a thick membrane, expands to fill the whole cell, leaving a thin membrane. This summons Godmind to emerge and resume control, for it is our natural state when living in higher states of consciousness. When functioning from Godmind all things are possible because we are free from mortal boundaries. We can, at will, consciously travel among dimensions and choose to take our body along or not.

Many minds are out-of-control with thoughts jumping back and forth like rabbits across a field. Thoughts arise as an opposition to life. We try to control the seeming unpredictability of events by relating to or anticipating them. We encumber ourselves with the weight of self-reflection rather than innocently experiencing the moment. Thoughts pull us out of the present into the immediate past or future causing energy to drain out of one pole or another. This results in losing lifeforce and becoming subject to aging and death.

We cannot ascend until we quiet our minds. That process may feel like a battle because our Higher Self wishes to be in charge but the surface mind guards its supremacy with fiery determination. The left-brain will feel threatened and fight any thought that doesn't support its world views.

By aligning the minds, the mental body ceases to be a barrier to the outer three bodies and we are able to access our life's blueprint.

The center of the Medicine Wheel contains both the above and the below. The color of the earth below is green. The color of the sky above is blue. So the center is the blue and green combined, which is turquoise. That is the secret behind why many Native Americans frequently wear the stone turquoise.

Earth has Three Minds

The earth also has three minds. These correspond with the three main chambers in the Great Pyramid in Egypt: the underworld is her subconscious, which is the Dark Chamber under the pyramid; the middle world is her surface mind, which is the Queen's Chamber; and the upper world is her Godmind, which is the King's Chamber.

Any fears and limitations we possess manifest in the Dark Chamber, which is why the initiate clears all fears during the spirals on the Medicine Wheel.

In the Queen's Chamber, we come to the world of light (left-brain) and shadow (right-brain). Hades is the name ancients called the shadow mind of the earth, which is similar to our right-brain. For entry into Hades, we are given a riddle and it can only be solved through right-brain by tuning into the heart.

We have to go from left-brain, where we predominantly live, through right-brain to get to Godmind, as represented by the King's Chamber. It is an inner map showing us how to merge the left and right brains to access the highest mind.

Mastery Below – The Subconscious Mind

The subconscious is a primitive mind. It is full of twisted views of life resulting from our painful experiences. It is like a receptacle that we stuff with fears and negative programming, "Naughty girl, don't do that. You aren't clever enough. Don't make noise. You aren't pretty enough. Don't go out without a sweater, you'll catch a cold."

If we focus on the past then we are predominantly living from the subconscious mind. This frequently results in despondency, suicidal tendencies and drug addictions.

The soul speaks to us through feelings. Our subconscious is located in the heart center. If this mind is cluttered with fears, doubts, and old programming, we may misinterpret the communication by accepting a feeling as pure when in actuality, it is prompted by negativity.

The subconscious connects our mind with everyone else's via the soul matrix next to the heart. Through this we are connected to the grid of humanity.

Balancing the minds is called the vertical alignment. The horizontal alignment is when the subpersonalities become balanced. The two are interconnected because the dysfunctional subpersonalities need to be healed before the subconscious is cleared.

By using the nine steps of releasing the past, the subconscious can become clear of the majority of fears and negative programming. If you find that some remain, the next step is to use rebirthing techniques. You may wish to use a professional[23] trained in rebirthing. This offers more immediate results since it is guided.

---

23 Leonard Orr has successfully trained many rebirthing practitioners.

We can apply rebirthing techniques ourselves. Its advantage is a slow and gentle release. The key is to give ourselves time to process the emotions that come up. If we stuff them down again, it doesn't work. Allow yourself time to cry, be afraid, angry, etc. Let your inner adult talk the inner child through his trauma.

'How to' exercise: The best method to access the trauma we experienced at birth is to submerge the body in a tub of water. Adjust the faucet to trickle warm water into the tub to maintain a comfortable temperature. Have a timer nearby and set it for 30 minutes.

Breathe in at a rate that is comfortable. (The emphasis is always on drawing the in-breath.) Without any break between the in-breath and out-breath, relax the breath out. Without any break, inhale again. Then relax the breath out. Repeat for 30 minutes. If you experience an overwhelming urge to get out of the water, in all likelihood, you have reached a threshold. If you remain five minutes longer, the major things will probably surface. Another approach is to apply the breathing exercises while walking.

Please note–It is critically important not to hyperventilate. It should be a comfortable breathing process.

This style of breathing promotes longevity, so you may wish to practice it until it becomes your normal breathing pattern. Remember to place the emphasis on the inhale.

Rebirthing techniques commonly relieve stuttering and other breathing disorders because grief and past-life trauma is usually held in the lungs.

Unresolved issues filter down to the subconscious of creation, the same as it does in our minds. Third-dimensional earth is the subconscious of the cosmos, so that makes us the inner child of creation. Therefore, the unresolved mysteries of the Cosmos has filtered down for us to resolve in our lives that the One may be enriched by the insights gained through the many.

Mastery Middle–The Surface Mind

We need to look at why creation was formed to understand why our left-brain (conscious mind) and right-brain (unconscious mind) became separated.

The Infinite formed creation to examine the unknown aspects of itself. With this intent, Archangel Michael (Mi-ka-el) undertook the first act within creation. His task was to gather together all that was known (the light) and separate out everything else, which was designated the unknown (undeveloped light). This resulted in creation receiving a left and right brain, one to deal with the known and one for the unknown. This is how duality formed for us, too, because we are the micro-cosmos of the macro-cosmos.

Races were designed to play the masculine and feminine aspects of creation, so that through experience, these mysteries could be explored. The function of the masculine was to separate out the various components for the sake of analysis. The function of the feminine was inclusiveness: to include the unknown within the known. The feminine gathers all it can about the unknown and delivers the information to the left-brain for interpretation.

There is a delay between cause and effect due to the density on this planet. This time lapse precipitates loss of perception, therefore, instead of pure discernment as its means of analysis, the left-brain became dysfunctional and started judging.

The left-brain embodies the universal fear of annihilation that

213

comes from believing ourselves to be separate from the Infinite. Since it fears for its survival, it becomes fanatical about maintaining control. It suppresses any messages from right-brain that cannot be interpreted by using logic or bodily senses. Consequently, we become locked in a world that has lost its magic. No longer do we hear the whisperings of the wind or see the faun dance with wild abandon in the moonlight. No longer do we intuitively know the day the hummingbirds leave to fly south for the winter. No longer do we hear the siren song of the goddess as she beckons us into a world filled with wonder and mystery.

Using alchemy, it is through mankind that El-ka-mi transforms matter, through energy, back into light. In ancient tongues, the word "mi" is consciousness (which is light). The word "ka" is energy. "El"[24] stands for earth or matter. Archangel Michael (Mi-ka-el) was the one responsible for stepping consciousness (mi) with energy (ka) down to matter (el).

All initial energy goes to left-brain and excess energy goes to right-brain. The left-brain has usurped its position and wants to control everything. That uses the majority of energy. That is why it is of paramount importance to constantly watch the left-brain[25]. Remember, it is like a horse that wants to run wild but we have the reins. If we are trying to accomplish something and there is a lot of distraction, pull on those reins and command the mind to focus.

The sacred geometry of left and right brain is the equivalent of two soccer balls, or dodecahedrons, each with 12 facets in the shape of pentagons. However, the right-brain contains a 13th facet within. When all 12 facets have been brought into marriage between the left and right brain, the 13th pentagon within allows pas-

---

24 "El" in pre-Sumarian languages stood for lord.
25 To assist with mastering the mind, reference "Path to Freedom" I-III tape sets.

sage to Godmind. In other words, it is a doorway and the goddess holds the key, therefore, when she is suppressed we are barred from higher consciousness.

Goddess and God Archetypes

The goddess and god archetypes are luminous Beings that represent different aspects of the Divine, like the facets of a diamond. When called upon, each one draws in the energy for that specific aspect.

The 13 Goddess/12 God Archetypes

The First Goddess forms a bridge with other lifeforms. She has reverence for all life, therefore, she remains sensitive to the interactions between all beings. She can hear nature speaking and is in harmony with its cycles because she feels them within her.

The First God analyzes how mankind can sustain the race with the help of nature without disturbing its balance. He deals with earth sciences and analyzes what will enhance the productivity of the earth. He understands electromagnetic fields and how they respond to the sacred spaces and locations on earth.

The Second Goddess is the history keeper. She knows the history of people is kept in their bones and the history of the earth is kept in stones. She remembers and preserves history to ensure that the energetic channels of the earth, the laylines, remain open and flowing.

The Second God gathers information about the known and analyzes the lessons from past experiences. He reads history from geology and archeology. He learns lessons from ancient civilizations.

The Third Goddess uses our innate sense of justice to measure actions. She makes sure all beings are treated fairly. She will defend the helpless and vulnerable.

The Third God is the protector of the boundaries of individuals and society. He is the policeman and judge, making sure the boundaries are set and enforced.

The Fourth Goddess is the mystic. She accesses information through non-cognitive processes using pure feeling. She is the intuitive and she alters reality through using emotion and visualization.

The Fourth God analyzes the spiritual laws that govern the universe. His quest is to see symbolically and understand the truths hidden behind the illusions and symbols.

The Fifth Goddess provides guidance to others on how their life's purpose will unfold. She delivers messages that are coming from the ancestors. She is adept at interpreting omens.

The Fifth God analyzes the hidden challenges within problems. He gathers insights from experience. He prepares strategies to overcome weaknesses.

The Sixth Goddess is the guardian of the ancient, sacred tradition of story-telling and oral transference of information. She honors the power of the word and its ability to shape reality.

The Sixth God is a teacher. He allows students to learn through their own experiences. He devises analogies, metaphors and parables to assist people into effortlessly learning. He sees the value of humor in teaching techniques.

The Seventh Goddess understands the divinity of beauty and grace. She adds warmth and sensuality to life. She is the homemaker and takes care of the needs of the family. She loves without judgment.

The Seventh God discerns how compassion should be expressed to best benefit the recipient. He ensures that his loved ones are respectfully treated. He analyzes and nurtures weak areas of relationships.

The Eighth Goddess is in charge of death and birth. She

works with herbs and communicates directly with the spirits of the plants used for medicinal purposes. She is a healer and knows the use of ritual.

The Eighth God is responsible for male initiations and rites of passage. He works with the study of medicine, anatomy, botany and pharmacy.

The Ninth Goddess feels how actions will influence upcoming generations. She leaves them a heritage that nurtures growth.

The Ninth God is a goal setter. He measures progress by goals achieved. He possesses a strong survival instinct.

The Tenth Goddess is the artist and muse. She is spontaneously creative about finding solutions. She inspires others.

The Tenth God is a creative problem solver. He is the inventor who pushes limited vision beyond its boundaries.

The Eleventh Goddess honors the self. She promotes self-respect through praise. She nurtures individuality in herself and others.

The Eleventh God forges new paths to fulfill the yearnings of the heart. He provides leadership and endurance and is the guardian of impeccability.

The Twelfth Goddess celebrates accomplishments and designs ceremony. She lives in a state of praise.

The Twelfth God is the architect of pomp and splendor and creates order by developing hierarchy.

The Thirteenth Goddess is the door of everything[26]. She forms a passageway into Godhood through stillness of being. She is the guardian of the keys that unlock the gate between the known and the unknown. When all the other archetypes are expressing harmoniously together, she takes charge of the alchemical processes that

26 Odes of Solomon

will alter the body to prepare it for ascension.

'Note'–There is no male counterpart for the 13th goddess archetype. She is the one in the middle of the circle that is activated when all the other archetypes merge into one. (In indigenous traditions, these archetypes are related to the moons.)

Mastery Above – Godmind

Godmind accesses the unknowable and is located in the fields around the body as well as through the cellular matrix of the body—it is literally lodged in the cells. The unknowable is comprised of everything that cannot be accessed by either left or right brains or the subconscious. It includes many things that defy verbalization, for no language exists to describe that which is the unknowable. In some traditions, access into Godmind is called "illumination." It can come bit by bit or in an instantaneous lightning flash of disconnection with surface mind. When Godmind takes over as the governing force of physical life, the experiences of all the subpersonalities are discerned by the inner sage, who downloads it into Godmind. Godmind already knows all things pertaining to light, but our mortal experience is at the cutting edge and explores undeveloped light. Therefore, the sage's interpretation of human experience feeds Godmind with new information. As humans we are pushing the boundaries of that which is known.

"For every atom in our bodies is a peep hole into eternal space and every moment a doorway into infinity. When we obtain even a glimpse of the truth that 'I AM He who sent me,' love, praise and gratitude burst open the gates of the Holy of Holies within and Godmind comes forth. In this moment the King of kings once again resumes his rightful throne within our lives and we live at the apex of mind where the inner and the outer cosmos meet. Behold, we have become the door of everything."[27]

Five Stages of Godmind

The Opening of the Remaining Chakras–Physical symptoms precede the opening of the remaining chakras. These include: feelings of dying; heart palpitation as the balance between the kidneys and the heart is disturbed, and cold sweats resulting from adrenal hyper-activity. At times it feels as though we are falling backward over an edge, as though the breathing and heart are stopping. Our energy levels drop dramatically at this time. Then, in an instant, we have a peak experience and the other five chakras burst open, forming a total of 12.

Clairvoyants might be able to see the rare and glorious energy configuration around the body of a person who has gone through this stage, but subjectively, it might just feel as though you are walking in a state of heightened awareness.

Becoming the Observer–During this stage we feel as though we are watching our life's experiences as a spectator. The technique of not-doing becomes a way of life. The insight that becomes an integral part of our life is that we aren't our experiences. The energy level is still low but it is higher than the previous stage.

We feel removed from humanity and are starting to remember that although we choose to remain in character on stage, this is but a play. Our loved ones may find us more detached and less fun. Even as we are crying our tears and laughing our laughter, we observe these actions from afar. Our boundaries start to break

27 "Healers of the West Wind: Sacred Keys to Healing Power" by Almine

down and we become more allowing since we are in the preparatory stages of entering into God Consciousness, which only allows. We also experience less and less linear time. Frequently, we cannot remember the last few minutes. We start to carry notebooks to list tasks that must be addressed. When others try to commit us to future plans, we struggle to fit this concept into our minds. It isn't until the next stage that we see the future as many probabilities.

The Disconnection–This stage can come in an instant. Suddenly the individual feels "emptied out," which can be describe as a bucket of bolts turned upside down. We realize we are no-thing whatsoever and that there is nothing outside ourselves.

At times, and especially initially, it feels as though we are losing our mind. Indeed, we are because we are losing the functions of surface mind. Suddenly you cannot remember your own name and you might stare at it in confusion. Certain human concepts no longer make any sense. For example, I couldn't fit the word "forgiveness" into my vocabulary. Forgiveness implies guilt and I only saw the innocence of the human experience and realized there was nothing to forgive. All desires fall away and things that used to matter suddenly don't.

Although energy is more available due to the opening of the additional five chakras, it now plummets to an all-time low and outer activity slows down. We can hardly remember how to pick up a pencil, and fear, once again, rears its head. At moments we are so expanded we can hardly find our body and when we do, we feel terrified and claustrophobic by being so confined. Perhaps the most disturbing of all is the complete lack of emotion, since all desire has fallen away. During this stage, the voice assumes a flatter tone due to a shift in the assemblage point.

The two main challenges of this stage are that firstly, in the midst of loss of self-identity, self-awareness has to be maintained. Secondly, if we don't know this is a positive stage and a step forward, we may resist the disassociative feelings. The illusion of loneliness can be so intense that many ancient seers died of its melancholy. It is crucial to release any resistance to these feelings. Unless someone who has already walked this path informs us that it is necessary to surrender our resistance, it could prolong this stage, perhaps by up to 11 1/2 years, according to ancient texts. (In my case, this stage lasted a little over one year.)

The Stage of Bliss–The realization that we are no-thing during stage three shifts to the realization that we are all things. As a result, we experience continual bliss. Be careful not to confuse bliss with joy. Bliss isn't an emotion nor is it a feeling, but rather a vibration that filters through the cells. During one of my children's births, I was given heroin by a nurse in the hospital to curb the afterbirth pain. That is the closest earthly experience I have had that describes an inkling of what awaits in this period.

The effort of speaking during either the disconnection or bliss stage becomes cumbersome and may leave us drenched in perspiration. The difficulty in relating to others becomes heightened. You may also experience a change in breathing rhythms. Thinking becomes obsolete and effortless knowing takes its place.

Many regard the bliss as a point of arrival. However, it is important to remember we are on a journey back to the heart of God and there is no point of arrival.

Most masters never go beyond this stage because it is very easy to become addicted to the intoxicating bliss and slip into the pitfall which some ancient shamanic traditions call "old age" [28]. Unless we choose to move forward, it will result in stagnation because lit-

28 See "Traps and Pitfalls" section.

tle exploration of the unknown is occurring.

Staying in Character–We return to a stronger association with the body. It is a choice we make, with some considerable effort, to delve back into the human experience. We are choosing to stay in character, on stage, even though we fully understand it is a play. This helps us to interact with other people again. Yet this time we embrace their folly since we have seen the innocence and purpose of all experiences.

When we choose to engage in the human experience again, then joy (the desire to live) starts to re-appear. During the early part of this stage, I taught small groups of students as a means of re-engaging in life. I was reluctant at first because all I wanted to do was bask in the bliss. It was only in doing so that I was rewarded with growth and joy.

As we move through stages two to four, we began to lose contact with our subpersonalities, which is why our energy levels are low, our boundaries unprotected, and the concept of fun incomprehensible. During this stage, these pieces return, one by one, and yield memory of our past, which had fallen by the wayside.

How to Make Decisions

To the average, unaware person, the left-brain makes nearly every decision. These decisions are based on social conditioning and logic—the "shoulds" dictated by society.

Some tend to bypass the left-brain and make decisions based on their emotions. The joy we experience when we have done something that feels great is the inner child's way of confirming our choice. We need to be cautious about making decisions based on emotion because it could be the result of a dysfunctional inner child. The only time our feelings are trustworthy is when the subconscious has been cleared out and the inner child connected. Then the emotions can confirm our feelings.

Emotions have desire as their foundation. Once we move into the mastery level and start accessing Godmind, we recognize that we are all things, so desire drops away, taking the emotions with it. What we are left with is the ability to access pure feelings. As a consequence, we confirm choices using different techniques.

At this point we act only if it contains a lesson that will solve another mystery of our beingness. We don't search for it; we don't run from it—the future will take care of itself. All we do is live the present moment and observe the ripples in the tension of our spiderweb[29]. If 10 possibilities present themselves, we need not act until challenged by one that offers potential growth. It isn't a selfish motive to ask where we can learn the most because if we act on the highest choice, it will benefit everyone and everything around us.

We determine this by how many lines intersect one point on our personal spiderweb. Indicators in our environment represent the lines. For example, if you are wondering whether to choose a red or a white car and suddenly 10 red cars in a row drive by the car lot, this is an indicator. Perhaps several unrelated people desire for you to offer private counseling sessions. You trained for it years ago, but didn't pursue it as an occupation. You have wanted a part-time job but aren't attached to any one thing. You are waiting for guidance from Spirit to show you your next step. A few days later you bump into an old friend in the grocery store who is moving to Europe for six months. He has an office that will be vacant and offers it to you to use while he is gone. These are all lines inter-

---

29 The spiderweb of light extends out from our body in all directions across the universe. We use it as a map to expand and contract as we need to when we enter God Consciousness.

secting a common point.

When multiple lines intersect one point, then we choose to live the indicated point or not. If we accept it, we place that spot in the center of our spiderweb. Then we align the center of our spiderweb with the center of the universal spiderweb so everything we do is in accordance with the will of God.

When making decisions, it is helpful to know that each of the minds deal with a specific body of information. They do this through the subpersonalities (the warrior, adult and sexual persona are grouped together) gaining experiential knowledge that is then interpreted by its respective mind.

Information can be divided into the known, the unknown and the unknowable.

The Three Bodies of Information
The Known

The left-brain is responsible for accessing the known, which constitutes 1/12th of that which can be known by man without being in God Consciousness. It uses two tools for this task.

The first is not-doing. It is invaluable in helping us see the big picture because we lift ourselves above the circumstance to gain a broader perspective. It keeps us from becoming hung-up in details. Therefore, it is a tool for applying discernment while making decisions.

When not-doing becomes a constant mode of operation for the left-brain, we are embarking on the first stages of disconnecting from ego and entering into God Consciousness. Just prior to entering God Consciousness it feels as though we are observing our life through a tunnel, from afar.

The second tool left-brain uses in decision-making is seeing behind the appearances. It is the ability of left-brain to pierce the veil of illusion and see the essence of what is really going on. It teaches us to see symbolically, which prevents us from taking things at face value—a trap that could lead to incorrect decisions.

The subpersonality connected with left-brain is the warrior, which guards left-brain's thoughts diligently to ensure that it doesn't think limiting or dis-empowering thoughts that could create adverse circumstances. The sage has instructed the warrior that thoughts create reality and its job is to ensure that the reality produced by the thoughts is of the highest possible manifestation.

The adult contributes its experiences so that the logical mind can form deductions and file the information for future reference.

The sexual persona uses the physical merging with another to teach the left-brain to surrender its rigid grip on life so it can surrender to Godmind.

The Unknown

It consists of 11/12ths of that which can be known without entering Godmind. It is accessed by right-brain, which gathers information from other realms, the future, from unseen guides and allies, by intuiting motives and feelings from other people. It is also accessed by the subconscious that gathers information from our Higher Self and the collective consciousness of humanity.

The subconscious is the receptacle for the experiences of the inner child. It accesses truth with feeling and provides vital input for making decisions. For example, we meet a new person and we immediately experience a shrinking feeling. If we have recapitulated our past and know this person isn't reminding us of a former perpetrator, this feeling could indicate that even though strangers present themselves as friendly, they could be hostile.

The right-brain is where the nurturer downloads his or her experiences. For example, the nurturer may notice that the stomach muscles tighten every time you walk past an alley on your way to work. It reports this to right-brain who feels out the situation to aid you in making a clear decision. Could it be that somebody was killed in an automobile accident at this location? Is there potential danger in the future?

When right-brain, through being in an altered state, intuits this to be an unsafe place at some time in the future, it relays this information to left-brain, which logically concludes that a different route to work must be found.

The Unknowable

Godmind accesses the unknowable, which includes the majority of creation. When one enters Godmind, making decisions takes on an entirely different meaning. First of all, consideration about the future is very difficult to grasp because it isn't seen as one straight line but as many probabilities. The past doesn't exist, for one has entered eternal time by living in the moment.

The inclination is to only allow, especially during the first stages when the vastness of creation becomes part of one's mind. It is difficult at this time to make any decisions because we cannot find the voices of our subpersonalities. However, unless we do, we cannot bring the Divine fully into the flesh.

The sage gains insights from its interpretation of the experiences of its collective family, namely, the other subpersonalities. It downloads this to Godmind, and in this way, keeps Godmind connected with humanness. The temptation when entering into Godmind is to lose self-awareness. All self-identity is gone, but it is crucial to maintain self-awareness because it is our link to sanity.

Godmind is fulfilling the purpose of its Highest Self, which is a being as vast as the cosmos. Its decisions are made as follows: it lives in an expanded state of awareness and merely places its intent upon its wishes. Then all of creation moves to make it so. It doesn't have to think, for it recognizes that thinking takes too much energy. It effortlessly knows.

CHAPTER FIVE

MERGING WITH HIGHER SELF

Traps and Pitfalls

As we follow the path of ascension, there are a few traps and pitfalls we need to be aware of.

The Four Traps

Ignoring the Unknown

Anything that doesn't conform to an existing belief system is dismissed, ridiculed or attacked. "Oh, that didn't happen," is a common statement used in overlooking unexplainable events. For example, a woman saw a deva in my backyard. Since the idea of a deva didn't fit into her belief system she devised an elaborate explanation. A few minutes later she declared that it was an electronic hummingbird traveling along a wire.

Making excuses to dismiss the unknown is the pacifying of reason. Many people say they are seeking truth, when in actuality, they are seeking to confirm their existing world view. It may be expressed as ridicule, stating, "Spirit doesn't speak to you directly. That voice you channeled was the drunk who hangs around city hall each night."

Many are scared of anything they cannot rationally explain and that may come forth as an outburst of anger.

People hold on tightly to their belief systems. It is sometimes difficult for us to understand that a loved-one would rather die than be healed. If they were healed, they would be forced to change their belief system. At times it is easier for us to accept people clinging to their belief system if we realize it is all they have. It is their identity and they are prepared to die for it.

If we are busy arguing away the unknown, we fail to receive the lesson at hand and it may have been the one designed to push us to our next level of growth.

Thinking We Already Know

We cannot take the unknown at face value or we will fall into the trap of thinking we know. The future, people, and words are part of the unknown. For example, what we think people say is frequently not what they are trying to convey. Their truth remains hidden. This applies to a description of an experience as well. We may have had a similar experience but that doesn't mean we know what that individual felt or thought because he may have an entirely different world view than us. Approach the unknown by feeling the true meaning with your heart.

To the average person, trap number two provides a feeling of comfort. He thinks he knows everything. Even those who are open-minded may say, "I may not know everything, but I do know what isn't possible."

Obsessing About the Questions

Obsessively asking questions drains our energy. An example of this is the questions that may have occurred to the woman who saw the "electronic hummingbird": A deva? What kind of deva? How do we know it is a deva? Could it be something else? If they really exist, why is this the first time I have seen one? Do other people see them too?

Most of the universe is unknowable. If we obsess about the unknowable, we miss the mysteries revealed by being in the moment. If our mind is cluttered with questions, we aren't still enough to receive guidance and insights.

If we accept that we live in an incomprehensible universe then we stay open and flow with life. If an obstacle comes up, we flow around it. We have no expectations of the world. We are innocently experiencing life as we go along.

Giving Our Power to Guides

Lightworkers need to be careful not to give their power away. Over the centuries, we have given our power to governments, religious groups, bosses, parents and even lovers. Unfortunately, Lightworkers also give their power to guides and spirit helpers.

One man has a guide that tells him how to live. It says, "Don't let your son go out, his mother is going to call soon. Tomorrow your boss is going to want that paper you've neglected. I think you should take an umbrella, it is going to rain." This is interference, not assistance.

High-dimensional guides won't tell us how to live or make our day-to-day decisions. They will present options and light the way, but they won't interfere with our free will. Generally, they come when we seek them through prayer and ceremony, but they may appear unsolicited if the timing is urgent, such as an emergency. They won't rob us of our ability to make mistakes, since these mistakes are our greatest teachers.

Sometimes guides from lower dimensions tell us these things to make us depend on them because they feed on our energy. Information isn't a good exchange for energy since many guides will tell us what they think we want to know. It is crucial to understand that lower-dimensional guides can only tell us knowledge that already exists on the planet, meaning ultimately, we already have access to it.

Lightworkers are falling into this trap due to ego. It makes them feel important that someone comes to them for advice. People are attracted to channelers because they don't believe they can access the information themselves. Consequently, they seek answers through anyone who has any level of guidance. Sadly, they often blindly accept the information, never asking whence it came. It is okay for us to demand to know who is speaking to us, however, they often call themselves by a name that appeals to us. We can set boundaries and declare that only high-dimensional beings are allowed to communicate with us.

We need to exercise our intuition and apply discernment at all times, with all information. Don't take anything at face value and feel everything with your heart.

The Four Pitfalls

Fear

When we release ego identification and activate Godmind, we

realize we are all things, but before we fully grasp that, we will experience being no-thing. We find ourselves standing alone and it can be disconcerting the first time we realize, "I am nothing. I know nothing, and I live in nothing I can understand." This may put us in fear as we feel either too expanded or too contracted. This fear may feel like being in the bottom of an abyss and many Lightworkers will shut down at this point.

Another common fear is the unknown. Most people are afraid of change and if they are pushed too quickly, they may turn against the one they see as bringing change.

For example, a teacher can inadvertently do this. If he is delivering a higher level of information than the student is prepared to receive, the student may turn against the teacher rather than admit he isn't willing to take the next step. This also happens if a student hasn't released ego identification and the teacher prompts him toward a threshold and he doesn't succeed. If he has attachments to pride, his ego may be wounded and rather than try again, he may slander the teacher.

It takes great courage to embrace the unknown aspects of ourselves.

Addiction to Challenge

When we start to see behind appearances, we know that we contain everything within that we need to meet the challenges of life. These challenges alter our perception and perception yields the gift of power, so we may find ourselves seeking them with an attitude of "bring it on!" This is being addicted to challenge. After we release the addiction and deal only with the challenges that are truly the next step on our path, we gain an inner quietness and confidence. We no longer need to prove ourselves to anyone—not even our self.

Power

Within the challenge of power we reach the ultimate choice which is called the "road of high adventure". It is the place where we can perform great miracles. We have the ability to do showy things like making rattles fly or invoking balls of light to float around the room. If we become addicted to power by doing grand miracles, we become stuck. Many medicine men end up here because it is such an intoxicating place to be.

The other choice is to be humble enough to become a student again. This allows for growth. The student wants to go further because he knows power isn't the goal. It is merely a tool to facilitate our next step. To the student who possesses clarity, nothing short of the ultimate freedom from mortal boundaries will do.

Power has been described as one of the biggest pitfalls in the universe. If someone acquires power and doesn't have self-esteem, the temptation to abuse it is very intense. We cannot utilize power to obtain results that will benefit our personal intentions only, it has to be for the good of all. Remember, the universe won't entrust limitless power to those who haven't mastered themselves.

The lesson behind the test of power is that we don't use power unless instructed in the stillness of our mind and without attachment to results. That is the key. If we don't have attachment to results, there is no temptation to abuse power.

Relaxing into Old Age

Old age can happen at any age. It is when we have become powerful and sit back and feel we have arrived.

Many sages who have fully disconnected from ego and gone from the place of emptiness into the place of fullness, surrender to the bliss within. They allow themselves to sit next to horrific conditions and simply be. They prefer to be alone because in their aloneness they don't have to keep coming back to the human point of origin. In this state, the knowledge that "all is in divine order" may be taken to extremes. Examples of this include their not caring whether: they are alive or not; they sleep or don't; and whether they eat or not.

It is an enormous temptation to remain in that addictive place of bliss and cease human activity. The problem is the power we have gained fritters through our hands like sand and we lose it. Also, there is no impetus for growth.

Instead of sinking into complacency, if we make a 180-degree turn and plunge back into the human experience, we are able to slip past death. At this point, new lifeforce flows in, we reverse the aging cycle, and are set free from mortal boundaries.

The Three Gates of Ascension

The universe doesn't entrust limitless power to one who hasn't healed himself. For us to be able to wield power that could adversely affect other kingdoms, it is necessary that we have mastered ourselves and fully understand that in the eyes of God, all are equal.

Many shamanic traditions have tried to force their way into power using intense rituals, but there is a limit to the results these efforts can produce. There are no boundaries to one who perfects his or her character and seeks to become one with God.

As we climb the mountain of ascension we find ourselves going through three initiations. They appear as gates: the gate of love, gate of wisdom, and gate of power. Unbeknownst to the initiate, his Higher Self designs a series of tests to see if he has mastered certain perceptions. When he successfully proves himself, the universe bestows gifts on him. The trials designed to test our perception and the resulting gifts are what comprise an initiation.

The Gate of Love

The criteria for passing through this gate are the heart-felt recognition of the validity of every lifeform as a reflection of God. We must also fully understand that all of life is interconnected, meaning every overcoming enriches all life and every destructive act weakens the whole. Another aspect of interconnectedness is that our environment mirrors our inner state of mind (and it becomes a guiding force as one learns to read it).

This reverence towards life must be extended to our beloved mother, the earth. We need to acknowledge her sentience and cultivate a relationship with her. This ensures that we become aware of how our actions may effect her.

When this state of harmlessness has been achieved, the initiate may, without fully realizing, walk through the gate of love. He may have a peak experience but not fully grasp the ramifications. Nonetheless, a profound change has taken place and we may notice we are filled with empathy for the suffering of the earth and our tears flow for the suffering of man and disrespect to animals. We may even cry from being overwhelmed by the beauty of mankind and the world around us. Developing within us is a melting compassion because we know that behind the twisted emotions of others, lies the pain of alienation. This enables us to embrace the folly of mankind.

In light of this compassion that forgives all and the empathy that understands all, others spontaneously heal, and we find ourselves walking in grace: things effortlessly fall into place and animals respond differently to us because they know they are in the presence of love.

The Gate of Wisdom

To enter this gate, we have to be free from the traps that blind men. When we take things at face value, we fall into the trap of thinking we know. That blocks us from receiving new information and results in distorted perception.

We need to acknowledge that from our perspective, most of the universe is unknowable. That means we don't know the mystery of life. Those who grasp this concept are ever watchful to read the signs of the environment and wait with abated judgment until they receive the necessary information or insights. These people are free to receive the energy that would have been utilized to maintain their world views.

Words are another trap. Reason cannot hope to capture the essence of that which they describe, and they lull us into a false sense of understanding. When we understand that words can be deceitful, we start feeling other's words with our hearts, looking for the underlying meaning.

Another prerequisite to entering the gate of wisdom is inner silence. This is achieved by not obsessing about the questions. When the need to know has been silenced, the heart guides us with pure feelings that enable us to access the unknown. Recapitulation further silences the internal dialogue and within the silence, all is possible. Truth starts to reveal itself effortlessly when it is no longer barred by the fanatical activity of the left-brain trying to defend its world views.

Similarly to the gate of love, some who pass through the gate of wisdom may not understand what it means at the time it occurs. Others may be jolted by it. Either way, the results filter through one's life like gold dust that has been spread upon the wind. In quietness and in confidence, information pours forth into our consciousness. At this point, one is no longer an initiate but has passed into the level of an adept. Rational thinking requires a lot of energy, whereas effortless knowing doesn't. We will find that Spirit is whispering answers to assist with our next step. Since we can hear the Universe guiding us, we no longer feel alone. We stop seeking the meaning of life. We lie back in the arms of Spirit and the "peace that passeth understanding" enters our life.

The Gate of Power

The gate of wisdom provides increased energy that is now discharged to us in the form of direct power. The preceding gates prepared us for the enhanced perception necessary to use power.

The prerequisite for the gate of power is that we must become a perception seeker rather than a power seeker. As described earlier, the perception seeker has ceased to need and knows he is his own source of power.

One who isn't supported by his or her subpersonalities could fall prey to the intoxicating temptation to use powers for the aggrandizement of himself. That is why this gate is positioned close to the top of the mountain.

Once we have entered this gate we notice miracles occurring, instant manifestation of thoughts, and increasing synchronicities. However, there is a learning curve with miracles. At first, miracles are only visible to the performer. When we pass the test of not needing to persuade others for the sake of approval, our power grows and we can openly show a life of miracles.

We know that all power is within us. It only requires attention and intention to direct its course.

The Two Stages of Ascension

At the top of the mountain when the lightning flash of consciousness awakens us to the grand realization that we are all things, we look back with astonishment at how far we have come. Realization dawns that the journey that brought us to this point traversed two different terrains; we passed through Two Stages of Ascension.

Life Eternal

The first stage culminates in an insight that death has no hold on us. It is a result of painstakingly rejecting the world view that old age and death are a necessity. When we shed the past and balance our emotional components, we unveil that our birthright is joy. The joy awakens in us the Three Ascension Attitudes that change the vibration within the cells, like a new song being sung. This creates a noticeable change in the vibration of our body that can be physically felt. The new song of the cells replaces the old programming. We find that remnants of unresolved trauma from the past disappear. As mentioned in the scriptures, "the years eaten by the locust" are restored to us.

This cellular song of gladness has to mirror back to us in our environment. This frequently results in losing old institutions, such as friends, jobs, and other situations that no longer serve us. The fear that we might falter vanishes since ample evidence has revealed itself that we are walking in a state of grace. At this point, aging ceases for we have mastered the atomic elements of the body. If on a rare occasion negativity travels through our cells, we can physically feel the shock to our system. We may experience nausea, trembling and weakness to the degree that we may pass-out.

Life More Abundant

The second stage that is reached after we have passed through the gate of power is "life more abundant". It is a place of expanded awareness that knows it isn't the body. It has learned to love without pain, to work without attachment to outcome, and to see the perfection underlying appearances.

During this stage we have mastered not only the atomic elements, but the environment as well. The endocrine system of the body reveals its hidden qualities and we start to live beyond mortal boundaries.

The treasure chest of hidden gems has been opened, and one of its great gifts is that even the effects of our past "wrong-doings" are erased. All karma is removed since restrictions in the universal flow of energy no longer exist within the Seven Bodies. That means events attached to these constrictions also heal. In this way, we effect not only the future, but the past as well, and even those who have borne the consequences of our misperceptions benefit. At the apex of the mountain, we can come and go with the speed of thought and our life of miracles takes on an even deeper meaning.

Claiming Who You Are
Humility

Modesty doesn't belong with God Consciousness. Humility does. Humility isn't the misplaced modesty of thinking we are less than another. That is paying homage to another person's arrogance.

Humility is acknowledging that everyone, no matter what detours he or she may choose, is an expression of God. There are variances in the amount of consciousness we are expressing, but there is no distinction in value. The life of the mass murderer in the street is as valuable as a saint's life in revealing the mystery to the Infinite.

The second part of humility is acknowledging that we cannot possibly hope to know the totality of existence since the unknowable constitutes the vast majority of the universe. This frees us to explore the tiny speck of the unknown that is in front of us. We can do so confidently, armed with impeccability as a shield, while playing the game "as if" we know. Remember, the game is played to stall for time to allow us to gain the necessary information or insights so surprise doesn't drain our energy.

Speak as One with Your Godself

We need to make a final transition into speaking as one with our Godself. Beginners have a tendency to make elaborate explanations like, "By the grace of God, if He is willing, He'll work through me and you'll be healed." This follows the image of being the flute and God blowing His music through us. But without the flute there would be no music. If we don't claim our Godself, then by whose authority are we going to cast out demons or command a cancer virus to leave? If we truly believe that we are One with Spirit, it is a natural extension of ourselves to command, "Let there be Light!"

When we start to say, "I heal," the last two connections are made in our body that is necessary to metamorphous it into an ascended master's body. That means the I AM presence is awakened and this doesn't occur until we claim who we are and speak our truth. This doesn't mean we have to shout it from the rooftops. We can speak gently and infrequently, selecting only words that honor the god-goddess within. It is no longer to anybody's advantage to pretend to be less than who we are.

Power is Your Birthright

Don't be afraid of power. It isn't power over another; it is power over ourselves.

The alternative to taking up our power is acquiescing to the world view that says we should follow others like sheep. Fear of power was reinforced by the genocide of over nine million in the name of eradicating witchcraft over six generations. The majority were women and ten percent were even children. These people were labeled witches for simple acts such as healing a child's boil, birthing a baby, performing a ceremony in the moonlight, or expressing gratitude to a river. It produced a deep scar in our psyche so it is understandable that many are frightened of power [30].

Those of the undeveloped light have frequently taken sacred symbols and rituals and turned them upside-down. For example, the five-pointed star, with the single-point upward, accesses the White Brotherhood. The undeveloped light uses it with the single-point facing downward. We also tend to associate the unseen realms with the undeveloped light because they know how to access them for power. All realms are part of the Divine; it is man's intent that determines whether power is used for good or evil.

The word evil is live spelled backward.

Some merely want to live in harmony and service, but where God expresses, there is beauty, love, wisdom, and power. There comes a point in fulfilling our blueprint where power is, naturally, the next step.

To be powerful and effective in fulfilling the roles we have agreed to play is the highest service we can render. When we align

---

30 Past life memories of having been killed during this genocide further adds to this fear of power.

ourselves with the powers of the universe we can create miracles. To be able to produce miracles on the physical plane, we have to manipulate it in the hidden realms. Great miracles are at our disposal when the hidden realms become more real to us than the physical realm[31].

When we successfully work through the stages of the Medicine Wheel, we develop the tools necessary to come into harmony with our Higher Self. This, in turn, enables us to gain the tools necessary to access the Higher Self of the planet that is the realm of the ascended masters. Then we are able to access the Higher Self of the universe. We are like mountain climbers connected by a rope—all the way to God. That connection gives us access to all the potential that can be expressed in this universe. This is how mystics bring to life the magic and miracles that we label impossible.

Many teachers will come forth during the next few years with the ability to disappear and materialize objects in front of us. It is important that we aren't misled by what they do. Judge them instead by who they are. An impeccable teacher will guide you and show you how to live by the example of his or her life. He or she won't tell you how to live.

Some teachers want to foster dependency for financial reasons, plus it strokes their egos. Look closely to see if the teacher is stuck on the label of being a master and whether he or she has an agenda with the students.

Be cautious with words because they shouldn't be taken at face value. When presented with new information (including mine), use discernment and determine that which resonates in harmony with the song of your heart, gently allowing the rest to roll away like water off a duck's back.

31 Reference "Internal Technology" and "Traveling Between the Unseen Worlds" tape sets.

There are times when Spirit instructs us to pick up the sword, but it is never our idea. These times are extremely rare. I have been asked to unravel another's plan only a few times. It was done with complete detachment to outcome, knowing that if anything in my life needed to be unraveled, that it would occur as well.

Treat power like the emergency supply of food in the garage: it is there if we need it but it isn't part of the regular stock.

How powerful we are as Lightworkers is determined by how much energy we can gather and allow to flow through us. Power enables us to move our assemblage point, meaning we are capable of experiencing 32 separate worlds (holograms) which are available to mankind. If we go beyond those, we shape-shift into animals and other lifeforms[32]. These worlds are separated from us only by vibration.

The general world view has a huge misconception about power by believing that advanced races create externally. The opposite is true.[33] If a highly evolved being wants to travel, he spins light fields around his body and creates a moving disc of light. If he is cold, he regulates his internal thermostat. He chooses whether to obtain energy by consuming food or pulling it in directly from light. Since the internal body is clean, body odors don't form and dirt doesn't stick to him.

When we claim our power, we can change the course of history. We are powerful enough to program a peaceable transition and unconditional planetary ascension, where all people are taken along. We can create a life filled with grace and a safe future for humanity.

---

32 This practice isn't conducive to our becoming ascended masters. Only power seekers use it as the lower vibration of the animal leaves its residue with the person. With repetition, the residue builds up and lowers the person's consciousness.

33 Reference "Internal Technology" Part II tape set.

Service as a Master

From the ultimate state of being, our service is pure. That means we take our next step with no expectations and no attachment to results. We perform the task at hand with complete focus and attention to the moment, observing without judgment. This is living in meditation—the place of inner stillness, innocence, and power.

As Lightworkers our actions need to be frugal, otherwise we deplete our energy. When we are still enough to hear guidance from our Higher Self, we will be able to honor the rhythms of the universe—the periods of rest and activity. There is a day and a night. There is a season for planting, a season for growing, a season for harvesting and a season for rest. Even Jesus Christ took his disciples into the mountains to rest away from the multitudes.

When the unexpected comes, a master acts with self confidence—even if he stares death in the face. This way he remains clear to the last minute. Death is an ominous force stalking those who are unconscious, but to a master, it is his strength. He lives every day as if death is on his doorstep and since he is facing the worst, nothing else can scare him. This prompts him to live on the edge with a vibrancy of life so he notices everything and finds pleasure in simple things. A master is vigilant in anticipating problems but lives joyously in the moment, expecting perfection. In this regard, death becomes our ally because it reminds us of our probable demise and to begin living every day fully. This lifestyle is a great contrast to the majority who are living a half-dead existence.

As spiritual masters, it is important that we take our light into the world and live our truth. We are the monks without monasteries, and we need to live in the streets amongst the masses. Many have ascended while in seclusion. This time it is different. We are

245

clearing all our parallel lives and ancestral issues so that the planet can ascend. We have specifically designed life among the masses to do this because the density accelerates growth.

The interaction also allows us to have an effect on a greater number of people. We do this by the electromagnetic frequency we emit. When others come in contact with this energy field, it causes limitations or constricting beliefs to instantly manifest. In this way it creates a potential environment for mental, emotional, or physical healings to occur. An example of this is when the woman touched the hem of Jesus Christ's robe and was healed. This happened as people were shoving him, yet he was able to feel her vibration of faith move through his body.

When everyone's limitations start manifesting, the outward appearance seems chaotic. Interpreting an event as chaotic is merely a lack of perception because when viewed from a higher perspective, it is a lower order destructuring to emerge as divine order.

The majority of people seem to be busy searching for something to come in from the outside, yet that yearning is for unity with our Higher Self. When reached, our human awareness that has separated, once again returns to wholeness.

A Parting Message

That which I undertake in great humility is but a reminder of the knowledge already contained within you. The lives of the thousands that have come to me for healing over the years have woven a thread into the tapestry of my life, rich and multi-hued. They have molded me into what I have become, and now I pass this sacred accumulation of knowledge on to you that it might form a golden thread in the tapestry of your lives.

The sublime path of being a blessing to mankind—to shed light on dark days—isn't for those who would feign ignorance in order to escape culpability. It isn't for those who would hide behind false humility, which is simply conceding to the arrogance of another. It is instead for men and women willing to let their light shine forth, increasingly, to illuminate with the soft glow of hope the darkest corners of the lives they touch. It calls for masters with the innocence of a child who freely acknowledge their inability to know the infinite plan of wisdom that has shaped their fellow man's life. For it is through these that God speaks.

There are those who greedily grab at every scrap of information, never pausing to incorporate it into their lives. They hoard and store and study knowledge as though by the mere knowing of it they could gain power. Book volumes of information cannot enrich those who aren't home for themselves by doing the work within. Yet men and women who have made wisdom their own, will find their lives altered by a simple phrase. It is to these that I speak. There are several layers of underlying information and the reader will find that as he grows, these will reveal themselves with each reading.

It is my sincere desire to share the continual stream of knowledge I receive through other books that build on these teachings. There is no end to the knowledge that can be brought forth upon our planet, but it must be called forth through a human heart.

In November 2000 I entered into God Consciousness and in me there remains no desire to know, but simply to be. In the grand design of things there is no difference in the importance of the one that turns the key versus the one who is the key. The ultimate goal is that the gates of knowledge be unlocked. I honor, therefore, your part in calling this book forth.

The love I feel for you is infinite and beyond words, for in your faces is mirrored the glory of God and within your lives the Divine is made manifest.

Excerpt from
"Healers of the West Wind: Sacred Keys to Healing Power"
by Almine

Closing Prayer

We ask for the courage to break through any limitations of perception that prevent us from being all we can be. May we earn the personal power to set us free from mortal boundaries; to rise like the phoenix from the ashes of disappointment and to pierce the veils of illusion that have obscured from man the possibility of his Godhood. To Thee the glory, forever and ever.

Amen

Additional Teachings by Almine

HEALERS OF THE WEST WIND
Sacred Keys to Healing Power
by Almine

An Amazing Source of Healing Wisdom,
Providing a Rare Glimpse into the Ancient Mysteries

"This beautiful young woman, whom I have come to think of as my daughter/friend, approaches life with respect, honor, compassion and communication—both speaking from and listening with her heart. These are the traits of a true healer."

Grandmother Nagi
Whiteowl, Native Elder

"Almine is a spiritual being of knowledge, truth, and light—a shining star of wisdom—with abilities no less than extraordinary. Her powerful message should be shared by all."

Linda L. Brown, B.A., N.D.,
Doctor of Naturopathic Medicine, Canada

"I am most impressed. I have never met anyone who knows better what it means to heal than Almine, medical doctors included. Our interactions leave me enriched."

Robert Jacobs, M.D. Medical Doctor, England

"Almine's genius lies in her extraordinary sensitivity to the energy fields of others. This gift makes her an exceptional healer."

James Alexander, D.C., Chiropractor, U.S.A.

"Almine fully lives her teachings and is the embodiment of pure love. I have been profoundly transformed by her compassion, and I unconditionally and highly recommend her teachings."

Kristayani Nancy-Jones, European Osteopath, D.O., France

"Almine is an exquisite teacher—exciting, uplifting, renewing. The heights of her teachings touch the depths of our souls—gently and delightfully effecting transformation."

Mary Cosgrove Staffa, Ph.D. Clinical Psychology, U.S.A.